Lindsay Mathis

What Do I See?

Program Authors
Richard L. Allington
Camille L. Z. Blachowicz
Ronald L. Cramer
Patricia M. Cunningham
G. Yvonne Pérez
Constance Frazier Robinson
Sam Leaton Sebesta
Richard G. Smith
Robert J. Tierney

Instructional Consultant
John C. Manning

Program Consultants
Jesús Cortez
Robert E. Slavin

Critic Readers
Anita A. Ayala
Anne H. Ferrell
Pamela B. Houlares
Jesse Perry
Charlene H. Romero
Patsy K. Vittetoe

Scott, Foresman and Company

Editorial Offices:
Glenview, Illinois

Regional Offices:
Sunnyvale, California
Tucker, Georgia
Glenview, Illinois
Oakland, New Jersey
Dallas, Texas

Scott, Foresman Reading: An American Tradition   Gold Medal Printing

Acknowledgments

Text
Pages 9–13: "Why the Possum's Tail Is Bare" by James Connolly from *Ranger Rick*, April 1985. Copyright © 1985 by the National Wildlife Federation. Reprinted by permission.
Pages 19–27: From *Send Wendell* by Genevieve Gray. Copyright © 1974 by Genevieve Gray. Reprinted by permission.
Pages 29–31: From *Everything Changes* by Morris Philipson. Copyright © 1972 by Morris Philipson. Reprinted by permission of Pantheon Books, a division of Random House, Inc.
Pages 32–40: From *Grandpa, Me and Our House in the Tree* (text and photographs) by Barbara Kirk. Copyright © 1978 by Barbara Kirk. Adapted and reproduced with permission of Macmillan Publishing Company.
Page 42: "Lemons and Apples" from *Woody and Me* by Mary Neville. Copyright © 1966 by Mary Neville and Ronnie Solbert. Reprinted by permission of Pantheon Books, a division of Random House, Inc. and Mary Neville Woodrich.
Page 69: "Secret Pocket" by Ilo Orleans. Reprinted by permission.
Pages 70–75: Adaptation of "Chipmunk Crossing" by Rita Marie Herther from *Highlights for Children*, October 1984. Copyright © 1984 by Highlights for Children, Inc., Columbus, Ohio. Reprinted by permission.
Pages 76–81: Adaptation of *My Friend Jacob* by Lucille Clifton. Text copyright © 1980 by Lucille Clifton. Reprinted by permission of the publisher, E. P. Dutton, a division of New American Library and Curtis Brown, Ltd.
Page 123: "The Dance" by Mildred D. Johnson from *Ebony Jr!* Volume 6, No. 6, November 1978. Copyright © 1978 Johnson Publishing Company, Inc. Reprinted by permission of *Ebony Jr!* Magazine.
Pages 124–133: Adaptation of the *Bremen-Town Musicians* by Ilse Plume. Copyright © 1980 by Ilse Plume. Used by permission of Doubleday & Company, Inc.
Pages 152–158: From "Rabbit's New Neighbor" by Margaret Meacham, *Highlights for Children*, December 1984. Copyright © 1984, Highlights for Children, Inc. Columbus, Ohio. Used by permission.
Pages 166–171: From "Experimental Growing Systems" and "People Behind the Scenes" from *The Land* sponsored by Kraft at Epcot Center. Reprinted by permission of Kraft Inc.

continued on page 296

ISBN: 0-673-74406-X

Contents

3

Why Possum's Tail Has No Hair

A Cherokee Folk Tale
by James Connolly

Many, many years ago, Possum had a
long tail. He would comb and brush the
hair on his beautiful tail. He was so proud
of his tail that he combed it every morning.
When the animals had a dance, he made up
a song about his tail. Rabbit, who had no
tail, thought Possum was too proud. She
wanted to play a trick on Possum.

Soon, there was to be a dance, and all the
animals were to be there. It was Rabbit's
job to tell the news to everyone.

Rabbit stopped at Possum's house to ask
him if he would be at the dance. Possum
said yes, but he would come only if he
could have a special place to sit.

"I have such a beautiful tail," he said. "I
need to sit where everyone can see me."

Rabbit said she thought that would be
fine. Then Rabbit said she would have
someone come to comb Possum's tail for the
dance. Possum was very much pleased.

Rabbit ran to see Cricket. Cricket was a fine hair cutter. Rabbit told Cricket to go the next morning and get Possum's tail ready for the dance. She told Cricket just what to do.

In the morning, Cricket went to Possum's house. "I have come to get you ready for the dance, Possum," he said.

This pleased Possum very much. He sat down, put out his tail, and shut his eyes.

Cricket began to work on Possum's tail. First he combed it. Then he cut off all the hair. As he cut, Cricket tied red bows around the tail to hold the loose hair in place. Possum, with his eyes shut, didn't know what Cricket was doing.

That night Possum went to the dance. A special place was ready for him just as Rabbit had said it would be. When Possum's turn came to dance, he stepped out, smiling.

Possum began to sing, "See my beautiful tail! See what a fine color my tail is!"

As Possum danced, everyone shouted. Possum knew they were shouting about his beautiful tail. So he took off the first bow to show his tail off very well. Then as he danced around singing all the bows came off.

Everyone started to laugh. They laughed so long that Possum stopped dancing and looked around the circle. The animals were laughing at him! He looked down at his tail.

Possum saw that there was not a hair left on his tail. He was so sad he could not say a word. He shut his eyes and played dead.

That is why Possum's tail has no hair, and why he plays dead when he is surprised.

1

How Do We Change?

We grow and change every day. Today we do things we could not do before. In what ways might we change?

The people and animals we know grow older and change too. In what ways might they change?

Each day we learn things. Animals learn things too.

Read about growing, changing, and learning.

Understanding What Happens and Why

Your old clothes may look funny on you. Do you know why this happens? It is because you are growing, so your clothes may look smaller.

Pat is seven. She has learned to play ball very well. Because she plays ball well she was picked first to play.

In the sentences about Pat something happened—Pat was picked first to play. Why was she picked first to play? Because she plays ball well. Clue words are words like *so* and *because* that may help you know what happens and why. Knowing what happens and why will help you understand what you read.

Read the next story to find out what happens to Jan and why.

Jan likes to read. Because she reads fast, she reads many books each week. Jan lives close to the library, so she can walk there.

Monday Jan didn't go to the library because she was sick. Jan wanted a new book to read, so she asked her mother to go to the library for her. Jan's mother brought home a great book for Jan to read.

1. Jan can read many books each week. Why?

To answer, find the word *because* in sentence two. *Because* is a clue word. It helps you know why something happened. Jan can read many books because she reads fast.

2. Jan can walk to the library. Why?

To answer, find the word *so* in sentence three. *So* is a clue word. It helps you know why something happened. Jan lives close to the library, so she can walk there.

3. Why didn't Jan go to the library on Monday?
4. Why did Jan ask her mother to go to the library for her?

Practicing Cause and Effect Relationships

Read the story to find out what happens to Spot and why.

Spot is Pete's pet rabbit. Spot is sad because he is left alone during the day. One day Pete teaches Spot how to hop over a stick. Now Pete brings his friends to see Spot do the trick, so Spot isn't alone.

1. Why is Spot sad?
2. What happens to Spot at the end of the story? Why isn't he alone?

Tips for Reading on Your Own

- As you read "Send Wendell" look for the clue word *so* to help you find out what happens in the story.
- Look for the clue word *because* to help you find out why something happens.

SEND WENDELL

by Genevieve Gray

Wendell lived on the top floor in a big
building. He lived with Mama, Papa, William,
Alice, James, Julie, and baby Anthony.
Mama and Papa and the children all liked
each other and everybody laughed most of
the time. But in a family there is always work
to do.

"Alice," Mama would say, "go over to Mrs.
Turner and borrow a cup of milk."

"I can't right now," Alice would say. "My
friend is coming to pick me up. Send Wendell."

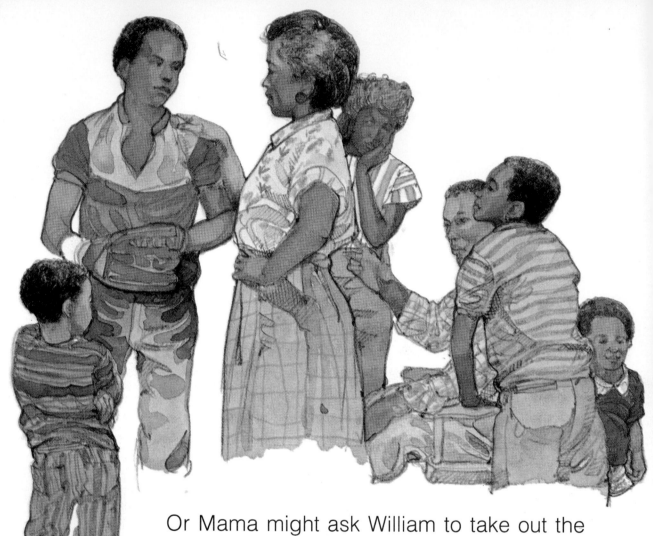

Or Mama might ask William to take out the trash.

"I have to play ball," William would say. "Send Wendell."

Or Mama would give James money to go for a loaf of bread.

"I'm too little," James would answer. "Send Wendell."

Wendell liked to help Mama, but sometimes he wished that William, Alice, Julie, and James liked to help as much as he did.

Early one Thursday morning, Mama said,
"Julie, go see if there is any mail."

"I have to put my doll to bed," said Julie.
"Send Wendell."

So Wendell went down to the mailbox.
There was a letter. He took it to Mama.

"Uncle Robert is coming to see us next
Thursday," Mama said with a big grin.
"Think of that! All the way from California!"

Wendell knew about Uncle Robert. He had
a farm in California. But California was
far away. No one in the family had ever
seen Uncle Robert but Mama and Papa.

The days went by and the family got ready
for Uncle Robert. Wendell did the most to
get ready, except for Mama.

"Alice," said Mama, "I'm busy. Take the
baby out, but be careful not to go far."

"I'm busy too!" said Alice. "Send
Wendell."

Early Thursday morning Mama said,
"William, go around the corner to the
cleaner's for me."

"I have school work to do," William said.
"Send Wendell."

So Mama gave Wendell the money.

"Be careful," Mama said.

Wendell went down to the first floor. By
the door was the biggest man he had ever
seen. The man was reading the names on the
mailboxes. He turned and looked at Wendell.

The big man began to laugh, just like
Mama.

"You must be James," he said.

"No, I'm Wendell," said Wendell.

"I'm your Uncle Robert," said the big man.

Wendell began to feel nice inside. The
nice feeling came out all over his face. He
could feel the corners of his mouth turn up.

"I have money and I'm going to the
cleaner's for Mama," he said.

"You are a good boy to help out," said Uncle Robert. "I'll give you a ride."

"You never saw your grandpa, did you?" asked Uncle Robert.

"No," said Wendell.

"When you grow up you are going to look just like him," said Uncle Robert.

Because Wendell could feel that nice feeling again, the corners of his mouth turned up more than ever.

Uncle Robert asked about each one in the family. Wendell told a little bit about everybody. Uncle Robert listened and smiled.

When Wendell and Uncle Robert got home, everyone talked at once and jumped up and down. They were happy to see Uncle Robert.

That night everybody ate dinner and listened to what Uncle Robert had to say.

Wendell just sat there and smiled.

Early the next day, Uncle Robert took the entire family to the zoo. And the day after that, they took a long bus ride.

During the visit, Uncle Robert told Mama and Papa about his farm in California. His children were growing up, he said. They all wanted to go to work in the city, so Uncle Robert needed someone to help on the farm.

At last it was time for Uncle Robert to go
back to California. Wendell was wondering if
he would ever see him again, when Uncle
Robert said, "Wendell, your Mama and Papa
say when you finish school you can come
help on the farm. Would you like that?"

"Yes," said Wendell. And he held Uncle
Robert's hand.

The day after Uncle Robert left, Mama
said, "Alice, take this plate back to Mrs.
Wilson."

"I just got home from school," said Alice.
"I'm busy. Send Wendell."

But Wendell smiled. "I have to write a letter to Uncle Robert," he said.

So Mama made Alice go.

Wendell got a pencil and paper. At the top of the paper he wrote in big, careful letters,

Dear Uncle Robert,

Meet the Author

"Send Wendell" is by Genevieve Gray. Genevieve Gray did many things before writing books. First she had two children. After they grew up she was a teacher for ten years. Now she writes books.

Genevieve Gray likes to write books that are fun. She wants there to be fun things in each of her books for children to read about and enjoy. Some of the books she wrote are *A Kite for Bennie, I Know a Bus Driver, Keep an Eye on Kevin,* and *The Seven Wishes of Joanna Peabody.*

Comprehension Check

- 1. What happens when Wendell's mother has a job for someone to do?
- 2. Why do the corners of Wendell's mouth turn up?
- 3. Why will Uncle Robert soon need someone to help him on his farm?
- 4. What do you think will happen the next time Mama has a job for someone to do?
- 5. Would you like to help on a farm? Why or why not?

See your Thinker's Handbook for tips.

- Comprehension: Cause and effect relationships

Communication Workshop

Talk

This story ends with a letter Wendell is going to write. Talk with a friend. Name three things Wendell might write about.

Speaking/Listening: Cooperative learning

Write

Imagine that you are Wendell and write a letter to Uncle Robert. Share your letter with your friend.

Writing Fluency: Letter

28

Everything Changes

by Morris Philipson

PART 1: Sometimes the sun shines
Sometimes it rains
PART 2: Sometimes the wind calls
Sometimes the snow falls

PART 1: Seeds grow to roses
to carrots to trees
PART 2: From eggs will come eagles,
turtles, and bees

ALL: Everything changes all of the time

PART 1: Dogs were once puppies
Cats little kittens
PART 2: Frogs were first tadpoles
Hens little chickens

ALL: Everything changes all of the time

GIRL: Especially people!

PART 1: Whether they're poor
or have lots of money
PART 2: Whether they're sour
or cheerful and funny

BOY: Thick, thin, short, or tall
People change the most of all

PART 1: Some who are SAD
can become very HAPPY

PART 2: Some who are DULL
can become rather SNAPPY

PART 1: Just as a storm
in a rainbow may end

PART 2: So can a stranger
become your best friend

ALL: Everything changes all of the time
And That's Just Fine

Grandpa, Me, and Our House in the Tree

by Barbara Kirk

My name is Nico.

Early next Thursday my grandpa is coming to visit me. Grandpa and I are perfect together. He likes to do all the things I like to do. That's what makes his visits extra special.

Grandpa even plays the flute. Sometimes I try to make the sound of the flute with my voice. One day I will take flute lessons. Then Grandpa and I will play our flutes together.

Grandpa and I love to run and play ball.
The two of us even made a tree house.

When Grandpa last visited, my mom took
pictures of Grandpa and me.

Early Thursday we start to get ready for
Grandpa's visit. When Mom leaves to pick him
up, Dad and I make up the bed. Dad is not
smiling. He sits down a moment and says,
"Grandpa has been very sick. It's even hard
for him to walk or talk. You, Mom, and I will have
to give him extra help this visit."

"I don't believe it!" I tell Dad.

I remember that Grandpa is big and strong. He was the first one to climb my apple tree. He even climbed up carrying wood. I can't ever believe he is sick now. I feel a knot growing inside of me. It can't be true about Grandpa being sick. It just can't be true.

But if it is true, will we still have fun together? Will Grandpa still help me with my school lessons? Will we ever climb up to the top of the tree house together? Will we do things like play with my dog Hudson? Will Grandpa and I still share secrets? Will we still be perfect together? I feel awful! I don't know what to believe.

At last Grandpa is here! His face looks very white. He smiles a gentle little smile. "Hello, little Nico," he says.

Hudson runs over. He loves Grandpa too. But when Grandpa does not play with him, he looks sad and crawls away.

Dad puts one hand under Grandpa's arm. Grandpa waves to me with his other hand. Then they walk in the direction of the house.

I watch a moment as Grandpa and Dad walk away. I still feel that awful knot inside of me. I don't know what to do. I have not said anything to Mom about it. But I can tell that she is thinking about Grandpa too.

When I go into his room, Grandpa just shuts his eyes. He does not say anything. Everything is so different. I sit in a corner of the room. Grandpa and I have not spoken. Still, I think he knows I am here.

Soon I feel very alone. I walk outside. I don't even know in what direction to walk. I just walk.

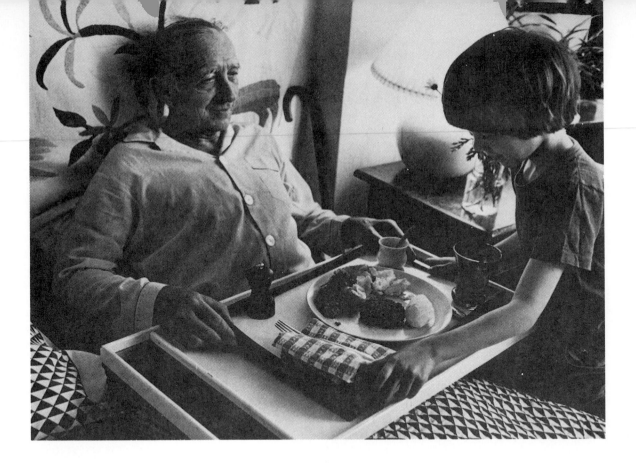

Later Mom asks me to take Grandpa his dinner. I try to make everything the way Grandpa likes it.

He sits up and takes my hand.
"Hello, Nico," he says with a grin. "Have you made any changes in our tree house?"

"Oh, Grandpa, you know I have been waiting for you to come and help me."

He smiles for a long time and says, "You must be the big builder now. I can't climb up, but I can still help you. I'll give directions. You carry them out. It will be fun."

Grandpa looks at me for a moment. Then he says, "By the way, do you need a telephone in the tree house?"

"A telephone? There is no telephone out there," I tell him.

"I know," Grandpa says. "But we can make one. We can make telephones from two cans and a piece of string. Then we can always talk to each other, even if you are in the tree house and I am down on the ground. Save the next two cans of dog food you open for Hudson. I will give directions so you and I can put together our own special telephones."

I crawl up on Grandpa's bed and give him a gentle hug so he knows I love him.

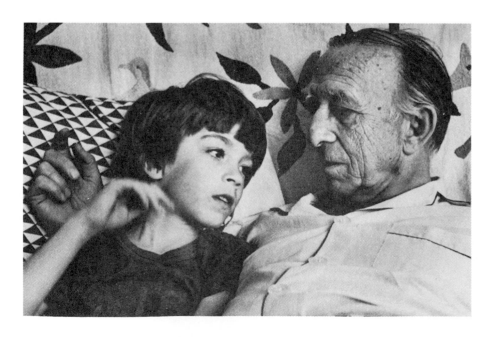

I give Hudson an extra can of dog food.
Now I have the two cans for our telephone.
I ask Mom for the longest string she has.

But the next day, and for many days after,
Grandpa stays in bed. He still has to rest.
So I paint the cans—one blue and one white.
The two colors are perfect together, just
like me and Grandpa.

Many weeks later, after all the leaves are
off the trees, Grandpa says, "I am feeling
better now. Early Thursday we can go out
and put up our telephone."

I don't feel awful now. I am so happy, I
feel like singing. Grandpa and I walk outside
and get to work.

Grandpa gives directions and helps me use the hammer to make a hole in each can. I follow Grandpa's directions and put the ends of a long string through the holes. Grandpa ties a knot inside one can, and I tie a knot inside the other. We see if the knots are strong. The knots are tied just right. At last it's ready.

I climb the apple tree with my end of the telephone. Grandpa waits near the tree. Our secret code word is Mississippi. I start, "Missis—" "—sippi," Grandpa finishes. Mississippi! It comes across loud and clear. I love Grandpa. We are perfect together.

Mom comes and takes this picture of Grandpa, me, and our house in the tree.

Comprehension Check

Think and Discuss

1. How did Nico's grandpa change?
- 2. How does Nico feel when he first sees Grandpa?
3. Why do you think Nico feels so alone and goes off by himself?
- 4. How does Nico feel after they have made the telephones?
5. Do you think Nico would be a good friend? Why or why not?

● Comprehension: Time sequence

Communication Workshop

Talk

Nico and Grandpa make a telephone. Talk with some friends about what other things Nico could do to let Grandpa know he loves him.

Speaking/Listening: Group discussion

Write

Draw a get-well card that Nico could give Grandpa. Write three sentences in the card that tell Grandpa how Nico feels. Share your card with your friends.

Writing Fluency: Get-well card

Lemons and Apples

by Mary Neville

One day I might feel
Mean,
And squinched up inside,
Like a mouth sucking on a
Lemon.

The next day I could
Feel
Whole and happy
And right,
Like an unbitten apple.

Animal Training

by Joanne E. Bernstein

Training animals is a long slow job.
Trainers begin when the animals are young.
They teach the animal one thing at a time.
They must teach the trick again, and again,
and again. Then the animal can remember it.

As it learns, the animal grows to love and
trust its trainer. It takes a long time, sometimes
years, for an animal to do a trick easily.

To teach an animal a trick there are a number of steps a trainer follows.

1. Say the clue words to the animal.
2. Show the trick, repeating the clue words.
3. Have the animal do it herself.
4. Reward her for doing a perfect trick.
5. Repeat the trick over and over.

 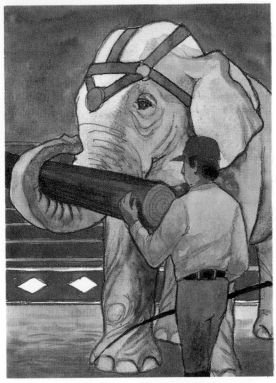

Elephants start their training when they are young. They begin at about three or four years old. The first trick an elephant learns is to answer to its name. To teach this, the trainer keeps saying the elephant's name. The elephant is rewarded each time it behaves right. The trainer pets the elephant and rewards it with a treat.

Animal trainers pick tricks that use what an animal can do easily. An elephant can hold things with its trunk easily. So it learns to pick up things with its trunk.

Trainers work in teams to be safe. One trainer watches the animals as another trainer works with them. One trainer always faces the animals and watches everything they do. The trainers move and walk the same way each time. This helps the animals trust the trainer. Training is safer when the animals trust the trainer.

Bears begin training when they are young, less than two years old. The first thing a bear learns is its name. Then a bear learns to stay in one place. Bears can learn how to pedal bikes and stand on their hands.

Horses can pick things up with their mouths easily. Trainers turn this into different tricks. Horses can take a carrot out of a trainer's pocket. They pick a card from their trainer's hand.

A trainer can teach a horse to pick a special box, take a flag out of it, and wave the flag. The trainer does the trick in many steps. Each step is repeated many times until the horse does the step easily and can remember it. The trainer rewards the horse each time it does a perfect trick. The horse remembers that it will get a treat if it behaves in the right way.

Here are the steps for teaching the flag trick to a horse:

1. Place three small boxes on a table. Put a treat under a flag in one box. Say a clue word. The box is small, so the horse has to take the flag out to get the treat. The horse needs to repeat this many times.
2. Take away the reward from under the flag. Say the clue word. The horse must take out the flag and hold it. Then give the horse the treat.

3. Close the top of the box. Say the clue word. The horse has to use her nose to open the box. She must pick out the flag and hold it by herself. Then give her the treat.

4. Show the horse how to wave the flag. Then for the final step she must wave the flag herself when the clue word is said before she is rewarded.

If you see an animal do a trick easily, you will know how much work it really is.

Comprehension Check

1. How do animal trainers pick the tricks they will teach?
- 2. Put these steps in order.
    a. Show the trick, repeating the words.
    b. Say the clue words to the animal.
    c. Reward the animal.
    d. Have the animal do it herself.
3. Do you think training animals is a safe job? Why or why not?
4. What animal would you like to train? Why?

- Comprehension: Steps in a process

Communication Workshop

Talk

Talk with a friend about animal trainers. Choose three words that tell about a good animal trainer.

Speaking/Listening: Discussion

Write

Write three or four sentences telling what a good animal trainer is like. Add your sentences to a class book about animals.

Writing Fluency: Sentences

LOOKING BACK

Thinking and Writing About the Section

See your Thinker's Handbook for tips.

| Prewriting |

You read how people and animals change. You can write sentences about what you like the most to share with your class. Copy the chart and fill it in.

	How does each change?	What do you like about him?
Wendell		
Grandpa	gets sick and better	
Nico		
horse		

| Writing |

Pick a character. Write three sentences to tell who he is, how he changes, and why you like him. Use your Writer's Handbook if you need to.

| Revising |

Read your sentences to a friend. Did you tell what you liked and use complete sentences? Make changes, proofread, and write a clean copy.

| Presenting |

Share your sentences with the class. Who picked the same character you did?

2

What Is Special?

Something that is special makes you feel good. What is special can be a place you have been or a thing you have. It can be something you can do or a thing you want. Anybody you know can be special. What is special to you?

You will read about special times and places, special friends, and special needs.

Learning About Setting

It was late at night. The waves splashed on the rocks. The sand was cold and wet. The boat rocked in the water.

Can you picture this?

No one was in the classroom. The tables were clean and in place.

Can you picture this?

When you read a story, it will help you understand what you read if you picture the setting of the story. The **setting** is where and when the story takes place.

Read to find out about the settings for Squirrel and John.

It was winter. The trees had no leaves.
Food was hard to find. Squirrel looked at
the food he had put away for the winter.
He did not want to run out of food before
spring. He knew that all during the
winter, he could only eat a little so it
would last.

1. When does the squirrel eat only a little?

To answer, look at the last sentence.
Winter tells you the setting.

2. Do you think Squirrel would have to only
   eat a little if it were not winter?

To answer, read each sentence. If it were
not winter and the trees were green,
Squirrel could find food. He would not have
to think about running out of food.

John was playing in the sand by the
sea. He made an elephant out of sand. A
wave came and took it out to sea.

1. Where is John playing?
2. Would a wave have washed away John's
   work if he had not been by the sea?

Practicing Story Elements: Setting

Read about Susan to find the setting, where and when, the story takes place.

Susan looked out at the audience. It was the first night of the play. Susan was afraid. The audience waited for the play to begin. There wasn't a sound.

Susan walked out on the stage. She opened her mouth. Nothing came out! She couldn't remember her words. Susan closed her eyes and thought. At last she remembered. She opened her eyes and said the words. The next time will be better, she thought, now that I know I can do it.

1. What is the setting?
2. What words are clues?
3. How does Susan feel as she walks out?
4. Why does she feel this way?
5. Will Susan be different the next time?

Tips for Reading on Your Own

• As you read "Lights Out" and "Beth Can Do It," picture the settings, where and when, the stories take place.

Lights Out

by Carla Rivera

"I'm excited!" I said. "This is my first camping trip. My first time in a tent."

"Ana, we left early so we will have time to explore the campgrounds before we eat," said Aunt Maria. She had the maps on her lap and read the directions to Mom. Soon we were far out of the city.

Mom began singing, "There's a bee, there's a bee, there's a bee on a tree." Aunt Maria and I joined in.

We went singing along, passing farms and houses. Soon there were no houses, only trees. At last, we came to the campgrounds.

We walked to a clearing down a path set off on both sides with white rocks. There were trees all around us. We watched the rocks so we would stay on the path and not get lost. Sometimes we had to walk around large rocks or trees that had fallen.

At the camp, other people were setting up their tents. Each family had a picnic table and a circle of rocks for a fire.

We set up our tent and went exploring down the path. I was feeling small among the giant trees. Everything looked so different without houses or stores as we would see at home.

By the time we got back it was dark. After dinner we put the dishes away and sat next to the fire. I was tired but really excited.

"Mom," I asked, "can we explore at night?"

"Great idea!" Mom said, "Get the light."

I took Mom's hand. Aunt Maria went first since she had the light. She pointed at a shape in the shadows and said, "The shadows of that fallen tree look like a giant bear."

"They do," Mom said. "And let's listen to the sounds of the night. It's not a bear, but I wonder what animal is making that awful, loud, calling sound?"

I could not see a thing. I hoped what was making the sound I heard was far, far away.

Aunt Maria started to say, "Look at that shadow over . . . ," but she didn't finish, because just then the light went out.

"We'll go back the way we came," Mom said. "Now that we can't see, we'll feel with our feet to find the rocks that had fallen on the path, and don't forget there are rocks on the side of the path to help us."

"Let's hold hands. That way we'll stay together in the dark," added Aunt Maria.

I was really afraid. I hoped we could stay on the path since we could not see.

"Oh!" I heard Mom cry out. "I walked into a low branch and hit my face. Don't forget to hold out your hands to feel for branches, so they don't hit you too," Mom said.

"Wait!" I said. I had tripped and fallen. I got up, and the three of us began feeling our way again.

At last we heard voices. We called out for help and another camper came over with a light. Now I knew we were going to be all right. We borrowed a light so we could return to our tent where we had an extra light.

I never thought I would be so excited to see a little light.

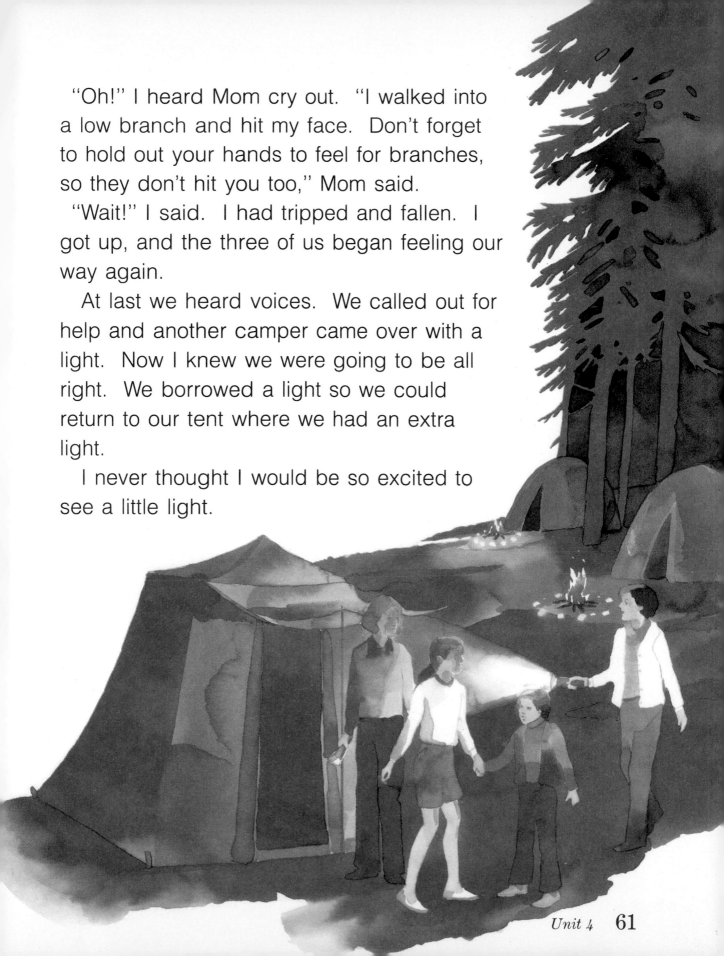

Beth Can Do It

by Sallie Rowe

Beth looked out the window of the spaceship. Chip and Dot, the robots, were at the computer, working the landing kit magnets. Beth called to them, "This planet does not look like Earth at all. I don't see any trees or flowers. I don't even see any people. What funny round buildings! What do you think lives in them?"

The robots came to the window and touched the computer. The door of the spaceship opened. Beth started down the steps.

But Beth did not go down. She went up. Beth was floating in the air. She caught the wing of the spaceship as she floated by.

"Help me, you two!" she called.

Chip and Dot reached out. Beth was too high! They could not reach her. "Hold on!" they called. "We'll get something."

They were back in a moment with a long pole and pulled Beth back into the spaceship.

"That was really something," said Beth.

"I should say so," said a voice.

"Who said that?" asked Beth.

"I did," said the voice again.

Beth and the robots turned and saw a big red eye looking in the door. Chip and Dot ran and hid behind the computer.

"Who are you?" asked Beth.

"Call me Raspberry," said the voice as a large, round, red thing with a green cap and one eye stepped in. "And who are you?"

"My name is Beth, and I come from the planet Earth," she said. "Chip and Dot, my robot friends, run the spaceship computer."

"How do you stay on the ground on your planet?" asked Beth.

"Look at my feet," said Raspberry.

"Oh, you have a special kind of magnet on your feet," said Beth. "Chip and Dot are made with special magnets, but I don't have any magnets. I float in the air on this planet."

"I'll tell you what," said Raspberry. "You come out with me, and I will hold you."

"Thank you," Beth said, holding Raspberry's hand and floating out the door.

Beth could not walk. Without special magnets she could not get her feet down. "I feel like a balloon," she said grinning.

"Floating is fun, but I really want to walk," said Beth. "Raspberry, will you take me back to the spaceship for a moment? I need the computer. I have an idea."

In the spaceship, Beth asked the computer for a very strong glue. Then Beth glued one of her shoes on top of Chip. Then she glued the other shoe on top of Dot.

"You are taking a long time," said Raspberry. "I hope your idea is good."

"It will be. You'll see," said Beth. "Now we are ready. Here we come."

Beth held the door of the spaceship. As the two robots came out, she stepped into the shoes on top of them.

"Come on you two, let's go," said Beth.

The robots' magnets worked. They stuck to the ground. Beth's idea worked! She did not float in the air.

"How do you like my idea?" Beth asked.

"Cute! My friends will want to meet the funny people from Earth," said Raspberry, looking at Beth on top of the two robots.

"Let's go see this planet," said Beth. "We'll have some story to tell back home."

- **1.** What is the setting for "Lights Out"?
- **2.** What words give you clues?
- **3.** Would the story have been different if An had not been exploring at night? How?
- 4. What problem did Beth have on the planet?
- 5. What other things might be different on Raspberry's planet?

See your Thinker's Handbook for tips.

- Literary Skills: Setting

Communication Workshop

Talk

Ana and Beth were able to visit a place the had never been before. Talk with a friend about the special things that happened to each girl. Tell how she might have felt.

Speaking/Listening: Discussion

Write

Be either Ana or Beth. List three words that tell how you felt on your trip. Write to a friend. Tell about how you felt on your trip. Use your three words.

Writing Fluency: Friendly letter

Secret Pocket

by Ilo Orleans

I have a very
Secret pocket.
And that is where I hide
So many things—
It's wonderful
They all can get inside.

A whistle, pencil,
Sticks of gum,
A skate key, rubber rings;
Some bottle caps,
A sheriff's badge,
And pebbles, crayons, strings!

My pocket must
Be *very secret.*
If mother learns what's in it,
Instead of being
Full, it would
Be *empty* in a minute!

Chipmunk Crossing

by Rita Marie Herther

Adam and David were chipmunks. They were good friends. They lived across the stream from each other. Together they had put a log across the stream as a bridge so they could visit each other. They visited every day.

Early one morning Adam heard a loud noise like a bump. He rushed to his window. He saw David taking acorns from the trunk where Adam stored his acorns for the winter. He saw David put the acorns in a sack.

Adam did not understand! Was David taking his acorns? David was Adam's friend.

Later, Adam crossed the log bridge to David's house and looked in the window. David was enjoying tea and acorns while chatting with another chipmunk. Adam knew the acorns were the ones David had taken.

Adam was disappointed! He was more than disappointed. He felt awful, and he was angry! Adam was so angry that he ran back across the log. Then he pushed and bumped the log until it fell into the stream.

"There!" he said and went home to sulk.

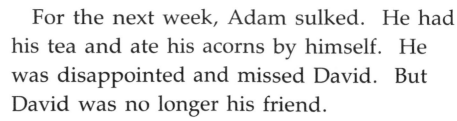

For the next week, Adam sulked. He had his tea and ate his acorns by himself. He was disappointed and missed David. But David was no longer his friend.

Then, early one morning Adam heard a bump and then a knock at his door.

"Hello," said a beaver. "I am looking for work. Do you have any work for me?"

"Yes, I do," said Adam. "Come in."

He told how David had taken his acorns. "I want you to build a tall fence all around my yard. And I want you to put a lock on the trunk where I keep my acorns. Can you do that?"

The beaver said, "Yes, I understand what you want, and I think I can help you."

"Good," said Adam. "I have to go into town for the day. You may begin the fence while I am away."

When Adam returned, he saw no sign of a fence. He looked at his trunk. There was no lock.

Adam was disappointed. "There must be some mistake," he thought as he sulked inside to make some tea.

While Adam was having tea, he heard a knock. Then David rushed in with a sack. "I knew we were still friends! I just knew it! My cousin came to visit me, " said David. "I was out of acorns. Since we are such good friends, I knew it would be all right if I borrowed some of yours while you were sleeping. I brought you new acorns."

David gave Adam the sack of acorns. "I saw you push our log into the stream," he said. "I thought you were angry because I borrowed your acorns. When I saw the new bridge, I knew you were not angry. I love your sign too."

Bridge? Sign? Adam thought. What in the world was David talking about?

After David left, Adam went to the stream. There was a beautiful new bridge. On the bridge, was a sign that read CHIPMUNK CROSSING.

Adam smiled. Yes, he thought, the beaver did understand what I wanted. It is good to have a friend.

My Friend Jacob

by Lucille Clifton

My best friend lives next door. His name
is Jacob. He is my very very best friend.

We do things together, Jacob and me.
We love to play basketball together. Jacob
always makes a basket on the first try. He
helps me to learn how to hold the ball so
that I can make baskets too.

My mother used to say, "Be careful with
Jacob and that ball. He might hurt you."
But now she doesn't. She knows that
Jacob would not hurt anybody. He would
never hurt his very very best friend.

I love to sit on the steps and watch the
cars go by with Jacob. He knows the
name of every kind of car. Even if he sees
it for a moment, Jacob can tell you the
kind of car.

He is helping me be able to tell the cars
too. When I make a mistake, Jacob never ever
laughs. He just says, "No no, Sam, try again."

And I do. He is my best, best friend.

When I have to go to the store, Jacob goes with me to help me. His mother used to say, "You don't have to have Jacob tagging along with you like that, Sammy." But now she doesn't. She knows we like to go to the store together. Jacob helps me to carry, and I help Jacob to remember.

"Red is for stop," I say if Jacob forgets. "Green is for go."

"Thank you, Sam," Jacob always says.

Jacob's birthday is two days before my birthday. Sometimes we celebrate together. Sometimes we celebrate with a party.

Last year we celebrated together. He made me a surprise. Jacob would stay in the house in the afternoon for a little while every day and not say anything to me when he came out. He would just smile and smile.

My mother made a cake with candles for me, and Jacob's mother made a cake with more candles for him. We sang, "Happy Birthday!" After we sang, Jacob smiled and handed me a card.

HAPPY BIRTHDAY SAM

JACOB

He had printed it all himself! All by himself, my name and everything! It was neat!

My very best friend Jacob helps me so much, I wanted to help him too. One day I decided to teach him how to knock.

Jacob will just walk into someone's house if he knows them. If he doesn't know them, he will stand by the door until someone sees him and lets him in.

"I wish Jacob would knock on the door," I heard my mother say.

So I decided to help him learn. Every day I would tell Jacob, but he would always forget. He would just open the door and walk right in.

My mother said maybe it was too hard for him. I felt bad because Jacob always helped me so much, and I wanted to help him too.

Sam's Room Please Knock

I would tell him and he would forget, so
one day I just said, "It doesn't matter,
Jacob, maybe it is too hard."

"What's the matter, Sam?" Jacob asked me.

"It doesn't matter, Jacob," was all I said.

The next day, we were eating dinner
when we heard this real loud knocking at
the door. Then the door opened and
Jacob came in.

"I'm knocking, Sam!" Jacob sang out.

Boy, I jumped right up from the table
and ran to Jacob. He is my very, very,
very best friend in the whole wide world!

Meet the Author

"My Friend Jacob" is by Lucille Clifton. She enjoys writing for children. She believes that it is good for children to feel good about things around them and to be proud of what they do.

While Lucille Clifton was growing up, her father told her about his family. It was as if he were writing a book. From her mother, Lucille also learned to love books. Her mother wrote a few books and read them to the children. Lucille loved to be read to.

Lucille Clifton now shares her love of books with her own six children. She gets many ideas for her books from her children. She enjoys writing about things that have happened in their lives.

The first book she wrote for children was called *Some of the Days of Everett Anderson.* Some of her other books are *Three Wishes, Boy Who Didn't Believe in Spring, Don't You Remember,* and *Amifika.*

Comprehension Check

Think and Discuss

1. What happens that makes Adam think David is not his friend?
• 2. How does Adam feel when he sees David having tea with another chipmunk?
3. What does Adam do to show his feelings?
• 4. How do you think Sam feels when Jacob learns to knock? Why do you think this?
5. How are Adam and David like Sam and Jacob? How are they different?

● Literary Skills: Character

Communication Workshop

Talk

Adam got angry at David. Sam says Jacob never gets angry at him or anybody. How do the characters show their feelings for each other? Share ideas with three friends.

Speaking/Listening: Group discussion

Write

Think about how the characters show their feelings. List three ways a friend can be a friend. Share them.

Writing Fluency: List

The New School

by Sallie Runck

CAST

MEG	WILL	FATHER
JOHN	BESS	A GOOSE
RUTH	MR. GREEN	TOM
STORYTELLER	MOTHER	

STORYTELLER: It is morning, many years ago in a small town called Pine Tree. The children are by a new schoolhouse.

MEG: Hello, Ruth. How do you like our new schoolhouse?

RUTH: I like it very much.

WILL: Did you know that my father gave the land for the schoolhouse?

TOM: Our mother and father gave the wood.

BESS: And my father helped to build it.

MR. GREEN *(coming to the door)*: Boys and girls, come in now.

STORYTELLER: The children go into the schoolhouse. Meg and John stop on the doorstep.

MEG: Did you hear that, John? Everybody did something for the new school.

JOHN: Not everybody, Meg. Probably just some people did things.

MEG: Well, I want to do something also.

JOHN: What do you think we can do?

MEG *(walking in the door)*: I don't know. I'll think of something, though. You'll see.

STORYTELLER: Everyone is in the classroom. Meg talks to Mr. Green and then sits.

JOHN: I wonder what Meg is up to.

MR. GREEN: Hello, everyone. I'm glad to see all of you. I want to thank your mothers and fathers for all the help they gave to make our new schoolhouse. Also, Meg and John will bring one more surprise.

WILL: John, what's the surprise?

JOHN: I don't know. Meg is up to something, though!

BESS: I hope it's good.

STORYTELLER: After school, Meg and John walk down the road with Ruth and Tom.

RUTH: Will you tell us the surprise?

MEG: I can't tell you now.

TOM: Come on, Meg. Why can't you tell us?

MEG: If I tell you, it won't be a surprise.

TOM: John, will you tell us?

JOHN: I don't know what it is either.

RUTH: Tom, I guess we'll just have to wait and see. Now I think it's time we go home. We have to help with the animals. **(TOM** *and* **RUTH** *walk on.)*

JOHN: Now will you please tell me what your surprise is?

MEG: I asked Mr. Green if there was anything we needed for the new school. He said we probably will need to have new quill pens. Goose feathers make good pens. Don't forget, we have that old goose, so for our surprise you and I are going to get quill pens for everybody at school.

JOHN: What a great idea, Meg! I know where we can probably find some feathers. Come on! Let's go to the pond.

MEG: We have to be careful, though. That old goose is mean.

JOHN: Oh, I'm not afraid of any old goose!

JOHN *(at the pond)***:** Look at these feathers, Meg!

MEG: I found some also!

GOOSE: Honk! Honk! Honk!

MEG: Look out, John.

JOHN *(shouting)***:** Go away goose!

GOOSE *(running at* **JOHN***)***:** Honk! Honk! Honk!

MEG: Run, John!

JOHN *(running while the goose chases him. He runs to an old wagon and climbs in.)*: Meg, get this goose away from me!

MEG *(**MEG** runs into the house, gets a pan of grain and corn and sets it by the house.)*: Here goose! Come and get it!

JOHN *(shouting from the wagon as the goose runs to the pan)*: Look at that goose go! It's a mean old goose and a fat one too!

MEG: Come on, John. If we hurry, we can get these feathers for the pens now.

STORYTELLER: John climbs out of the wagon. He and Meg collect more feathers.

STORYTELLER: Later, at the dinner table.

FATHER: You collected fine feathers. I think these will make good quill pens.

MOTHER: Did our goose give you any problems?

JOHN: Oh, just a little, but Meg saved me.

MEG: That old goose loves to eat.

JOHN: It's a good thing she likes grain and corn better than she likes boys.

MOTHER: Thanks to you two, everyone in your class will have one of these quill pens.

MEG: Thanks to that mean, old, fat goose too!

Comprehension Check

Think and Discuss

- **1.** What does Meg want to do?
- **2.** What does Meg decide to do to help the school?
- **3.** What does Meg do to get what she wants?
- **4.** Does Meg get what she wants?
  5. If you wanted to do something special for your school, what could you do?

● Literary Skills: Goal and Outcome

Communication Workshop

Talk

Talk with some friends about what schools were like many years ago. Think about what Meg and John might have done in school. What do you think you can do in your school that they could not do?

Speaking/Listening: Cooperative learning

Write

Imagine that you are able to visit Meg in Pine Tree. Write one page telling Meg things you have in your school she did not have. Read your paper to your class.

Writing Fluency: Description

LOOKING BACK

Thinking and Writing about the Section

See your Thinker's Handbook for tips.

Prewriting

You read about what can be special. Write a letter to a friend about what is special to you. Copy the chart and fill it in.

Character	What Was Special
Ana	
Beth	
Adam and David	
Meg	gave a special gift to school

Writing

Use the chart to get ideas about special things. Write a letter to a friend about something special to you. Use your Writer's Handbook if you need to.

Revising

Read your letter to someone in your class. Did you write about something special? Does your letter have five parts? Make changes, proofread, and write a clean copy.

Presenting

Mail or give your letter to your friend.

3

What Is Art?

We think of something as art because someone has taken time to make it look just right. When a cook takes extra time to make a plate of food look and taste special, it can be a work of art.

Painting, dancing, or music can be art. What art is in this picture?

Read about many kinds of art, people in art, and animals making music.

Understanding Main Idea and Details

Look at the picture. Tell what is happening. Is it about a yellow flower? Is it about a girl in a red shirt? Is it about a teacher? Is it about a drawing lesson?

The picture shows all of these things. But only one is the topic or most important idea of the whole picture. *Drawing lesson* is really what the whole picture is about. It is the topic of the whole picture.

You will understand more about what you read when you can figure out the topic and the main idea of a paragraph.

The **topic** tells in a word or two what a whole paragraph is about. *Drawing lesson* is the topic of the picture.

The **main idea** is the most important idea in the paragraph about the topic. If I put the idea in a sentence, I might say, "The class is having a drawing lesson." This is the most important or main idea.

Details are small pieces of information. What other details does the picture show about the main idea? They are learning to draw a flower. The teacher is showing the class how to use colored pens. There is a painting of a yellow flower.

Look for the main idea as you read about paintings. Find details that tell about it.

The class had an art lesson. The lesson was on how to draw different animals. During the lesson, the class used paints, clay, and colored pencils. After the lesson, they had an art show.

1. In a word or two, what is the topic?
   a. different animals   b. an art lesson

To figure out the topic, find the word that is used many times. *Art lesson* is the topic because the other sentences in the paragraph tell about the lesson. *Different animals* is only one detail.

2. Which sentence in the paragraph tells the main idea about the topic?

The sentence that tells the most important idea about art lessons is the first sentence. It tells that it was an art lesson. All of the other sentences tell details about the art lesson.

Turn to page 43. As you read the first paragraph, look for the topic and main idea.

1. In a word or two what is the topic of this paragraph?
   a. animal training   b. a trick
2. Which sentence in the paragraph tells the main idea about the topic?

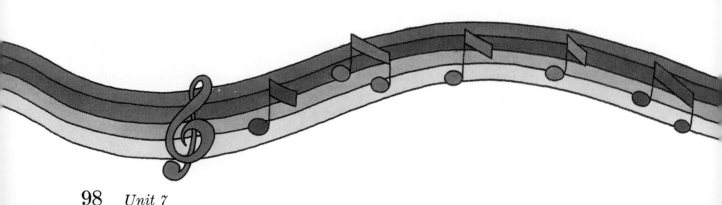

Practicing Main Idea and Details

Look for the topic. Read to find the main idea about the topic. Then find details about the main idea.

Music is art. It is the art of making sound. Music is beautiful to the ears, not the eyes. There are many kinds of music.

1. What is the topic of this paragraph?
   a. ears   b. music
2. Which sentence tells the main idea about the topic?
3. Which sentences give more details?

Tips for Reading on Your Own

- As you read "Art All Around You," find the topic. Look for an important word that is repeated in many sentences.
- Look for a sentence that gives the most important idea about the topic. It is the main idea.

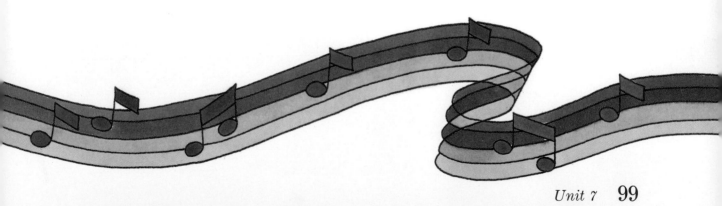

Art All Around You

by Carla Rivera

Art can be found in stores, theaters, zoos, or your own yard. Art can be made with a brush, a knife, a machine, or hands.

Years ago, stores used picture signs. Signs or rough wood figures told what the stores had. It was not wrong to use letters in signs, but paintings and figures were important because many people could not read.

Picture signs are still used. Very old signs have been put in museums.

Notice each photo. What does each photo tell you?

Masks are another kind of art. They are each planned, made, shaped, and painted to be something really special. They can be made from clay, wood, or paper. Hair and other things can also be glued on.

Have you ever wanted to put on a new face? You can. You can put on a mask.

People have been using masks since early times. Pictures on rough cave walls show us that people used masks to look like animals. The people hoped the mask would help them catch the animals they were chasing.

Masks are also used in the theater. People acting in plays use them. Masks are painted to appear happy, sad, or angry.

Masks have important jobs to do. Large masks can be seen even though you are sitting far away from the stage. Masks show different feelings. Special masks help a player's voice carry all around the theater.

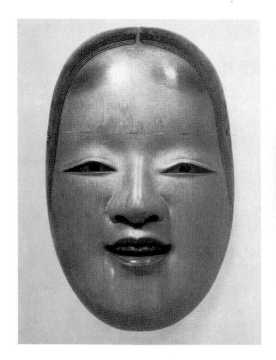

Theaters have other art. Painted settings tell where the story takes place. Acting is an art. Players cry and laugh as needed by the play. Their costumes are art.

Costume making is an important art. Costumes are used to tell a story. The color of the costume can be sad or happy. It can be new or old. Shoes can be high or low. They can be new or rough and old. Each part of a costume can tell about the play. The art of costume making means planning each costume just right. A player does not want to appear in a wrong costume.

Tree shaping has become a special kind of art. Trees that stay green all year are used. It is important to cut them many times during the year to keep their shapes. Then the animal shapes become a garden work of art. A horse and rider appear to be moving. It is the wind that makes them look that way. A bear or a dog appears in this garden art. Even trunks of trees are shaped.

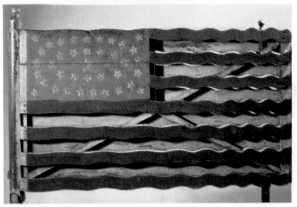

As you travel around, you may see other garden art. You may also notice art on fences and mailboxes.

How can machines become art? Notice the fence in the photo. Notice parts of machines, a knife, a pick, mule shoes, and wheels. What other things have become part of the fences in these photos?

Notice the photo of the flag fence. This flag was painted on wood and used as a fence. Now it is in a museum.

Years ago, if you traveled around a city, you would have seen weather vanes. Weather vanes, if made into shapes that appear extra special, are another kind of art. Many buildings had weather vanes. Even zoos had weather vanes.

Weather vanes came in many shapes and sizes. Some weather vanes were more than ten feet long. Some were round, some flat. Many had figures on them. Some figures were of animals, birds, or wheels. A ship was on one weather vane. The figure of an animal was on a weather vane over a zoo. What figures do you see in the photos?

  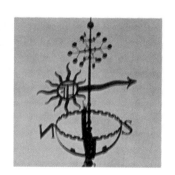

Some art is done with clay, a knife, sand, or paint. Some is done in snow. In winter, snow figures are made in many yards.

You can add many things to a snow figure. The nose can be a carrot, a stick, or coal. You can add eyes, hands, hats, and ties. Nothing is wrong when added to a snow figure. It is your work of art.

The scarecrow is another kind of art figure. There are even art shows of scarecrow figures. Prizes are given for the best scarecrow. Have you seen a scarecrow?

While you travel, even on your way home from school, look for art all around you.

Meet a Reader

Laqresha, a second grader from Ohio, likes reading. "I like to read books about animals. I take books out of my school library," she says. "In my class we read on a rug on the floor. Sometimes someone reads to us."

Laqresha also likes to go downtown with her mom and walk around and look in the many store windows. "It's fun to see all the different things," she says. "I like to look in the book stores and go to the big library downtown."

At school Laqresha painted a picture of the things she saw downtown. She likes to make things and enjoys art. She says if she painted a snow figure, she would use string for the mouth, a carrot for the nose, and little stones for the eyes.

Comprehension Check

See your Thinker's Handbook for tips.

Think and Discuss

1. Long ago, why was there art in store signs?
2. How did people use masks long ago? How do we use them today?
• 3. What is the topic of the paragraph on 104?
   a. green trees   b. tree shaping
• 4. What is the most important idea about the topic? Which sentence tells this?
• 5. Give three details that tell more about this main idea.

● Comprehension: Main idea and supporting details

Communication Workshop

Talk

Long ago, store signs had art to tell what stores were selling. With a group, name four kinds of stores. Talk about art that could help tell what each store sells.

Speaking/Listening: Group discussion

Write

Draw the art that best tells about one of the stores. Write sentences to tell why that art is best. Share with your group.

Writing Fluency: Sentences

109

Using Prefixes

Can you read the words in the pictures? Knowing the word parts will help you. The first word of each pair is a word you know. The second word has a word part added to the beginning of the word.

A **root word** is a word with no parts added to it. *Safe, hurt, even, pack, read, build, paint,* and *pin* are root words.

A **prefix** is a word part added to the beginning of a root word to make a new word. The prefix *un-* means "not" or "do the opposite of." The prefix *re-* means "again" or "do again."

Read about Joan's sign. Tell what each underlined word and its root word means.

Joan's sign was <u>unfinished</u>. She had to <u>remake</u> part of it. The sides had come <u>unglued</u>. She had to <u>rejoin</u> the sides.

To find the meaning for each underlined word, find its root word and its prefix. *Unfinished* means "not finished." *Remake* means "to make again." *Unglued* means "not glued" and *rejoin* means "to join again."

Practicing with Prefixes

Mary is <u>unhappy</u> with the way her picture looks. She will have to <u>redo</u> her picture.

1. What does <u>unhappy</u> mean?
   not happy   happy   happy again
2. What does <u>redo</u> mean?
   did   do again   not done

Tips for Reading on Your Own

- To figure out a new word, see if it is made up of a root word you know and a prefix.
- For more tips on figuring out words, see your Word Study Handbook.

The Flag of AMERICA

by Kim Franklyn Evans

Flags are a kind of art. A **flag** is planned to look pleasing and to stand for one thing like a group, a city, a state, or a country. A flag can have different figures, shapes, and colors. All these things put together well can make a flag a work of art.

Betsy Ross

The first flag of America was made in the year 1776 in Philadelphia. Many people believe that this flag was made by Betsy Ross. Betsy Ross had a small sewing shop in Philadelphia. People thought she had good ideas, used the best colors for each job, and sewed well.

The story of the first flag was first told in 1870 by her family. While there is no way to know, this story is believed to be true. Here is how it might have happened.

In 1776, Colonel George Ross, Robert Morris, and General George Washington visited Betsy Ross. She welcomed the three men into her shop. General Washington wanted her to make a flag.

Planning the Flag

General Washington explained to Betsy about the flag. He wanted one flag that would stand for all the groups of people that had come to America by that time. It was important for the flag to have one star and one stripe for each group. He also explained that the stars were to be in a circle. This would show that each of the groups was part of one **country**, America. The flag's colors were to be red, white, and blue. It was believed that red was brave, white was proud, and blue was strong.

The Stars for the Flag

George Washington had a drawing of the flag. When Betsy saw the plan for the flag, she was unhappy with how the stars looked. She noticed that they each had six points. Since Betsy's job was to know about art, she explained that the flag might look better with five-pointed stars.

Betsy planned out a new flag showing how it would look with five-pointed stars. The men liked Betsy's idea, and Washington decided to redo the drawing.

Sewing the Flag

Betsy Ross started to work on the flag. First she sewed the red and white stripes together. Then she cut thirteen white stars and sewed them on the field of blue.

Betsy Ross worked for many days and had to redo some of it many times. At last, she welcomed Colonel Ross, Robert Morris, and General Washington once again to her shop to show them the finished flag.

These men showed Betsy's flag to many people. A year later in Philadelphia, the people made it the flag of America.

Philadelphia Museum

Betsy Ross made many other flags. Her house still stands in Philadelphia as a museum. Many people visit her house.

The Flag Changes

The flag has changed since 1777. When the flag first appeared, it had thirteen stripes and thirteen stars. It still has thirteen stripes to stand for the first thirteen groups of people, but the number of stars has changed. As America grows, a new white star is added on the field of blue to welcome each new **state** to the country. By 1959, America had become a country with fifty states.

Jan Brett

by Anne Mazure

Jan Brett has won awards as a writer and illustrator of children's books. She is the illustrator of three books she has written herself. She is also the illustrator of many books written by other writers. A museum has had a show of her art.

Being an illustrator is hard work. Jan Brett spends a long time each day drawing. She works at home. She has a special room where she does her art work.

Jan Brett was drawing a big picture of a fair. She remembers it was one day in her first year of school. She started with rides and balloons. She did not redo anything. She just added to her picture. Soon it had people and animals. It had everything you see at a fair, but Jan Brett had never been to a fair. She remembers it felt as if she really was at a fair. It had become real to her through her drawing.

Jan Brett travels through her drawings. She believes you can travel with her by enjoying her art.

Jan Brett feels that each one who reads her books is special. She wants her art to speak to each reader. She hopes her art will help a reader spend more time enjoying a book, enjoying each page.

Jan Brett rewards her readers for looking at her art. She adds little touches, extra things, to make her art real for the reader. She wants each page to be beautiful. She wants her art to add to the story. She also wants the art to have a story of its own. Maybe it is because of this extra special touch that she has won illustrator awards.

Mrs. Brett's first job as an illustrator was for a story written by another writer. Her first book as both writer and illustrator was *Fritz and the Beautiful Horses.* She has won an award for this book.

Jan Brett feels you should enjoy art. "Never feel unhappy with a picture you have done," she says. "Enjoy it. If you do feel unhappy, practice and work at it until you can enjoy what you have done."

Comprehension Check

Think and Discuss

1. For what do the stars and stripes on our flag stand?
2. Why has the number of stars changed?
• 3. What is the topic of the first paragraph on page 119?
   a. Jan Brett   b. fairs
• 4. What is the main idea about the topic? Which sentence tells you?
5. Do you think being an illustrator is much work? Why or why not?

• Comprehension: Main idea

Communication Workshop

Talk

Jan Brett wants her art to have a story of its own. Talk with a friend about how her art tells a story.

Speaking/Listening: Cooperative learning

Write

Write a short story about the art on page 119. Tell where the children are and what they are doing. Share your story with the class.

Writing Fluency: Short story

To be read by the teacher

The Dance

by Mildred D. Johnson

The dance is an old and ancient art,
No one is quite sure of its early start,
But everyone loves a dancer's grace,
Good dancers are found most every place.

There are all kinds of dances to watch and do,
Folk, ballet, tap, to name just a few,
Some dance for a living,
Some dance just for fun,
Dancing's an art to please everyone!

The Bremen-Town Musicians

Retold and Illustrated by Ilse Plume

A very long time ago there lived an old donkey who had helped a miller for many years. When the donkey had become too old to carry large sacks of grain on his back, the man didn't want to keep him any longer.

Afraid of what might happen, the donkey took to the open road while he still had the use of his four legs. As he walked, he decided that since he had such a beautiful bray, he would travel to Bremen-town and join a band of musicians there.

The donkey had not traveled far when he noticed an old dog resting in the road as if she had run a long way.

"What's the matter?" asked the donkey. "Why are you resting?"

"Oh!" moaned the dog. "What is to become of me? Now that I am old, I am not needed. I have run away, but I have no place to go."

"You are welcome to join me!" said the donkey. "I am going to Bremen-town to be a musician. I will bray and you can bark and together we'll make beautiful music."

The dog was glad to go, so the two traveled down the road together.

Before long they came upon a cat moaning by the side of the road. She looked tired and very sad.

"What is the matter with you?" said the donkey. "Nothing can be as bad as all that!"

"Little do you know," moaned the cat. "I am getting too old to chase a mouse. Now that my eyes and my teeth are no longer good, I am not needed. I have run this far, but where can I go now?"

"Come with us," said the donkey. "We are off to Bremen-town to be musicians. Your singing would be most welcome."

So the cat joined them, and the three traveled on together.

   Soon the friends came to a farm, and there on
the gate was an old rooster. His crowing was
so loud, they stopped in their tracks and
looked at him.

   "Red-comb, stop your crowing!" said the
donkey. "Why are you making so much noise?"

   "This is my last time to crow, so I'm making
all the noise I can," said the rooster. "Now
that I'm not as young as I used to be, they
have decided to make me into chicken soup!"

   "Listen," said the donkey, "you are welcome
to come with us to Bremen-town. We can all
be musicians there. You have a fine crow. No
one would hear it in chicken soup!"

   So the rooster went along, and the four
animals went on their way.

The friends traveled on and on, but Bremen-town was still a long way off. That night the travelers found themselves in the middle of a great, dark forest and decided to stay the night there.

The donkey and the dog went to sleep under a large tree. The cat sat on a low branch. The rooster perched near the top of a tree. From there he could see for miles. As he looked around, he saw a bright light through the trees of the forest.

The rooster called down to his friends, "I see a light. There must be a house close by!"

"Then let's go there at once," said the donkey.

At last they found themselves in front of the house. Inside they saw a table with good things to eat. A band of robbers was enjoying their dinner.

The four friends thought of a way to get rid of the robbers. The donkey put his front legs on the window. The dog jumped on the donkey's back. The cat climbed up on the dog. The rooster perched on the cat.

Then they all made their music in their loudest voices. The donkey brayed, the dog barked, the cat gave out a cry, and the rooster crowed. In the middle of all this noise, all four animals jumped through the window into the robbers' house.

The robbers jumped up and ran screaming into the forest, afraid for their lives.

The four musicians were happy to have chased the robbers away. They made themselves right at home and ate as though they had not eaten in weeks. When they had finished their dinner, they blew out the candles and each found a place for the night.

The donkey went outside to sleep in some straw. The dog went to sleep behind the door. The cat went to sleep by the fire. And the rooster flew up on the roof.

After much time had passed, the robbers came out of their hiding place. When they saw the house all dark, they thought they had been chased away too easily. The head robber told one of his men to go back and look around.

Without a sound, the man went inside to light a candle at the fire. There he saw the cat's eyes in the dark and thought they were coals from the fire. But when he started to light a candle from them, the cat flew at him! Before the robber could reach the door, the dog jumped up and bit his leg. As he ran across the yard, the donkey hit him with his back feet. Hearing all the noise, the rooster gave a very loud crow.

The robber was so afraid he did not stop running until he had reached the others!

"Awful things live in that house! We must never go back," he shouted to the other robbers. And they didn't.

As for our four musicians, they didn't go to Bremen-town after all. They decided it would be a shame to leave such a beautiful house. They are still there today, making beautiful music under the stars.

Meet the Author and Illustrator

Ilse Plume is the storyteller and illustrator of "The Bremen-Town Musicians." She won an award as the illustrator of this story.

As a girl, Ilse Plume used most of her time drawing, painting, and putting on plays for her dolls and stuffed bears.

Her love for art stayed with her all through school. She now shares her love for art with all the children who read her books. Ilse Plume is also the illustrator of *The Velveteen Rabbit* and *The Story of Befana* which are books written by other people.

LOOKING BACK

Thinking and Writing About the Section

You have read about different kinds of art. Your class can have an art show and you can write an invitation to give to a friend. First, copy the list and add to it.

What Is Art?
1. weather vanes   5.
2. flags   6.
3. music   7.
4.   8.

Writing

Pick some kinds of art your class could show. Write an invitation to send to a friend. Use your Writer's Handbook if you need help.

Revising

Read your invitation to a friend. Did you tell who the invitation is for and who it is from? Did you tell what, where, and when the show is? Add anything you left out and make a clean copy.

Presenting

Take or send your invitation to your friend.

Books to Read

Today Was a Terrible Day
by Patricia Reilly Giff

Have you ever had a day when nothing goes right? If so, you'll like this book about Ronald.

No Good in Art by Miriam Cohen

The art teacher said to paint a picture of something you like to do. Read to find out what everyone in the class painted.

Opening Night by Rachel Isadora

How does Heather feel on the first night of her dance show? Follow her every moment and see.

Frederick by Leo Lionni

Every mouse in the field worked day and night to put food away for the winter to come. Every mouse except Frederick. What will Frederick do this winter?

4

Who Lives Next Door?

People who live near you are your neighbors. Who might your neighbors be? What do the people do? Are they farmers or city workers?

Animals are neighbors too. Chipmunks, dogs, and cats are neighbors. Can some neighbors live in trees? Can neighbors help?

You will read about different neighbors, and what some neighbors do.

Using Graphs

Sam is going to a new school. He needs help in finding places and things. On Monday, the first day at his new school, five friends helped Sam. On Tuesday, three friends helped Sam. On Wednesday, four friends helped Sam.

The graph shows what you just read about Sam. A **graph** shows things in a way that is clear to read and understand. On a graph, pictures can stand for things. The graph **key** tells you how many things each picture stands for. You can easily see how many friends helped Sam each day.

Number of Friends Helping Sam	
🚶 = one friend	
Monday	🚶 🚶 🚶 🚶 🚶
Tuesday	🚶 🚶 🚶
Wednesday	🚶 🚶 🚶 🚶

Use the graph to find out how many
neighbors live on Apple Street. Read the key.

Neighbors on Apple Street				
▲ = 2 neighbors				
Boys	▲	▲		
Girls	▲	▲	▲	
Mothers	▲	▲	▲	▲
Fathers	▲	▲	▲	▲
Pets	▲			

1. How many pets live on Apple Street?

To find the answer, first look at the key
for the graph. The key tells you that each
picture stands for two neighbors. Then find
the line that tells how many pets are
neighbors. There is one picture on that
line. One picture means two pets live on
Apple Street.

2. Are there more girls or boys on Apple Street?

Neighbors on Apple Street				
▲ = 2 neighbors				
Boys	▲ ▲			
Girls	▲ ▲ ▲			
Mothers	▲ ▲ ▲ ▲			
Fathers	▲ ▲ ▲ ▲			
Pets	▲			

To find the answer, find the line for boys. There are two pictures on that line. Two pictures mean four boys live on Apple Street. Then find the line for girls. There are three pictures on that line. Three pictures mean six girls live on Apple Street. Since there are six girls and four boys, more girls live on Apple Street.

3. For which two neighbors are the numbers the same?

4. Which are there the most of on Apple Street?

    a. pets   b. mothers   c. boys

5. How many mothers live on Apple Street?

Practicing Using Graphs

Use the graph to find out the kinds of jobs people do in Cross City.

Jobs People Do in Cross City				
👤 = 3 people				
Cook	👤			
Teacher	👤	👤		
Painter	👤	👤	👤	
Musician	👤	👤		
Gardener	👤	👤	👤	👤

1. What job has the most workers?
2. What job has the fewest workers?
3. What two jobs have the same number of workers?
4. How many painters work in Cross City?
5. Are there more musicians or cooks in Cross City?

Tips for Reading on Your Own

- You can use a graph to see things easily.
- On graphs, pictures stand for real things.

A Visit to Green Street

by Judith A. O'Donnell

   Green Street is home to many different
animals. It is a grassy place with homes, a
farm, and many trees. Come along to find out
about the animal neighbors and their homes.
If you are quiet and take a close look, you
will find many different animal homes!

Animal Homes on Green Street

You can find many animal homes on Green Street. The homes are made from mud, grass, or twigs. Some animals build their homes above the ground or in trees. Others have their homes under the ground. Homes are used for sleeping, storing food, and caring for young.

If you look on the branch of a tall peach tree, you will find a bird's **nest.** Birds make their nests out of straw, grass, and twigs.

What else might you see? You might see a mother rabbit and her bunny on their way home. Rabbits make their homes in grassy places where they can find food and hide their young. In the spring, rabbits eat grass and flowers. In winter, they eat the twigs and bark from trees near their homes.

When you pick up a rock or two, you might find many different bugs living under them. Finally, you might also see a tiny chipmunk. Chipmunks live under the ground in homes that have enough room to store food.

The Pond

If you are quiet as you follow the path, you will find other kinds of homes. Be careful. The ground is stony.

Look! A mother duck and her ducklings are happily swimming in the cool water. They must have a home near the **pond.** A pond is smaller than a lake and has still water. Ducks build their nests in the grassy land around a pond. The mother duck makes a nest out of twigs and grass. She lines the inside of the nest with some of her own feathers so her ducklings will have a nice soft home.

What else lives near the pond? Look over there! See that large, flat, brown tail showing above the water in the pond? It's a beaver! He is building his home from sticks and mud. He gets in and out of his home through a hole that is under the water. The part of his home that sits above the water is a dry, quiet place where the beaver sleeps.

The Farm

Many animals live on the **farm** on Green Street. A farm is land used to grow plants and raise animals. The family who lives on the farm takes care of their farm animals. The farmer grows corn, beans, and carrots. He also grows plants to feed to the animals. The family dog has a house in the yard. The dog and her new puppy have their names painted above the door of the house.

The Barn

A **barn** is one kind of home on the farm. Who lives in the barn? Let's go in and see. The inside is quiet and cool and smells of straw. The ground is hard and stony. Cows and horses live in the barn.

Cows and horses are helpful animals. Cows are helpful because they give milk. Horses are helpful because they do work on the farm.

What else lives in the barn? See the mouse running through the straw? It lives in the barn with the farm animals. Any dark place that is warm and quiet makes a good home for mice.

Pigs live in the barn, but you might see them outside happily rolling in the mud. The mud makes their thick coats feel cool on a hot day.

The Chicken House

The house across the yard from the barn is for the chickens. Outside of their house, the chickens poke at the stony ground with their beaks to pick up grain and corn.

Inside the house, each chicken has a nest made of straw. Chickens are helpful because their eggs are an important food for people.

The door to the chicken house is open. Inside, the farmer is happily looking for eggs in the nests. One of the farmer's jobs on the farm is to collect all the eggs. Each egg must be picked up with care.

You have visited many animal neighbors and have seen their homes on Green Street. Look near your home. Be quiet, keep your eyes open, and see what animal neighbors you can find!

Comprehension Check

See your Thinker's Handbook for tips.

Think and Discuss

1. Name three animals and their homes.
2. What does a duck use to build its home?

Use the graph to answer the next questions.

Number of Eggs Collected

= 5 eggs					
Monday	⬭	⬭	⬭	⬭	⬭
Wednesday	⬭	⬭	⬭		
Saturday	⬭	⬭	⬭	⬭	⬭ ⬭

• 3. How many eggs were collected on Monday?
• 4. When were the most eggs collected?
● Study Skill: Graphs

Communication Workshop

Talk

Talk with three boys and girls. Think about where you live. What animal homes could you find?

Speaking/Listening: Group discussion

Write

List three animals that live on your street. Write a sentence about each one. Share your sentences with your class.

Writing Fluency: Sentences

151

Rabbit's New Neighbor

by Margaret Meacham

One Friday morning last summer, Rabbit looked into the window of the house next door. It was true. Someone was finally moving in. Through the window she could see a big gray packing trunk, some cans of house paint, and some brushes. They had not been there the day before. Rabbit also saw a truck in front of the house. Rabbit looked for more signs of her new neighbor. But the summer sun was so bright that it was hard to see into the dark house.

Rabbit ran down the street. She had not gone far when she came upon her friend Gander. "Good morning, Gander," said Rabbit. "I believe we have a new neighbor. I looked in the window of the house next door for a moment, and I saw a big gray trunk and some paint and brushes."

"How exciting!" cried Gander. "Did you see anything else?"

Rabbit was in a great hurry to get to the market. "Well, the sun was very bright," she explained quickly. "I must be on my way now because I am late for work at the market."

Rabbit was gone before Gander could speak.

Gander had gone to the bakery. He thought about the big gray trunk, and figured that the new neighbor must be an elephant. He must be an artist since he has paints and brushes, and his son is very bright.

"Good morning, Badger," called Gander. "We have new neighbors. An elephant who is an artist, and his son who is very bright. I just bought two cakes at Squirrel's bakery. His friends and their wives all made something special for this summer sale."

Badger was still thinking about the new neighbors and asked, "Are there any more?"

"I believe he has more," said Gander, who was thinking about the cakes from the bakery.

Later that Friday afternoon, Badger had gone to Goose's grocery to buy juice, jam, beans, and oranges. On her way home from the grocery, she saw Claudia and Percy Porcupine.

"An elephant family is moving next door to Rabbit," Badger said. "The father is an artist. One of his sons is very bright."

Badger asked her friends if they would like half of an orange. Claudia took one of the halves and thanked her, but Percy was still thinking about the neighbors. "Where are they from?" he asked.

"California, I should think," said Badger, looking at the oranges from the grocery.

Badger ran off. Claudia and Percy had not gone far when they saw Rabbit on her way home from the market.

"We have heard all about your new neighbor," Claudia cried over to Rabbit.

"Yes," said Percy. "A family of elephants from California. The father is an artist, and one of the sons is very bright.

"I will visit them later," said Rabbit.

When Rabbit got home, she went next door with fruit halves to welcome her new neighbor. She knocked on the door, and was surprised to see a beaver answer. Beaver asked her in for some cold juice.

As they talked and shared the fruit halves, Beaver told Rabbit that he lived alone, that he used to be a letter carrier, and that he rode in from Philadelphia.

"You know, it's funny," said Rabbit. "I had heard that a family of elephants from California had moved in."

Then Rabbit added, "I heard that the father was an artist. I also heard that he lived with his wife and children. One of the sons was very bright."

Beaver and Rabbit laughed. Rabbit put down her juice and cried, "I wonder how these silly stories ever get started."

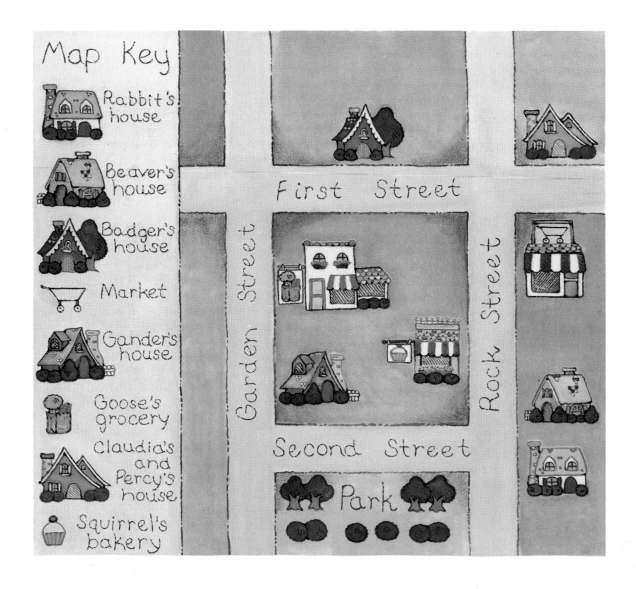

Map Key

Rabbit's house

Beaver's house

Badger's house

Market

Gander's house

Goose's grocery

Claudia's and Percy's house

Squirrel's bakery

First Street

Second Street

Garden Street

Rock Street

Park

Think and Discuss

1. Who really is Rabbit's new neighbor?
2. The animals make mistakes when they listen to each other. Which two mistakes do you think were the most funny?
3. Do you think the animals are good neighbors? Why or why not?
- 4. Look on page 158. Is Rabbit's house closer to the market or to Badger's house?
- 5. Who lives closer to Goose's grocery, Gander or Rabbit?

- Study Skill: Maps

Communication Workshop

Talk

Talk with your class. If someone new came to your school, what could you do to make him or her feel welcome?

Speaking/Listening: Cooperative learning

Write

Make a list of five things you could do to welcome someone new to your school. Put the list up for your class to see.

Writing Fluency: List

To be read by the teacher

Green Hill Neighbors

by Frances M. Frost

When I look at our green hill,
I think of all the wild
Small hearts that live inside it:
The woodchuck's chubby child,

Rabbits with busy whiskered faces
Peering out of rocks,
The big-eared meadow mouse, the dainty
Gold-eyed baby fox.

When I look at our green hill
Beneath the sunny sky,
I'm pleased to have such friends inside—
And glad I live nearby!

"Green Hill Neighbors" from *The Little Naturalist* by Frances M. Frost, published by Whittlesey House. Copyright © 1959 by the Estate of Frances M. Frost and Kurt Werth. Reproduced with permission by McGraw Hill Book Company.

Two Good Neighbors

by Charles David Raphael

This is about two good neighbors, Mary Ellen MacAndrews and Eldon Muller. They have different jobs, but both care about people. Both want to help other people.

First meet Mary Ellen MacAndrews, Billy's neighbor.

Mary Ellen MacAndrews—Neighbor

A small puppy ran past Billy and went under the table. It had a ball in its mouth. Just as Billy and his friends went to take the ball from the puppy, the puppy was gone.

Mary Ellen MacAndrews heard the noise. She looked over to her neighbor's yard.

"My new puppy is always running off with the ball," Billy said. "We can't play with the puppy in the yard."

"Come play in my yard," Mary Ellen said.

Mary Ellen MacAndrews—Teacher

Mary Ellen MacAndrews is a teacher. She teaches very young children to share and to get along with each other. She teaches them important school rules. She also enjoys art, games, and singing with the children.

Mary Ellen MacAndrews—Coach

Mary Ellen MacAndrews has another job. She doesn't get money for it, but this other job is one that's very important to her. She coaches a softball team. A **coach** is someone who teaches or trains others in a sport.

"I do it for myself as well as for the girls," she says. "I like to see the girls enjoy games. I have been coaching teams of young girls for about five years now. I made up my mind to coach the young girls myself. I teach them early to enjoy softball.

"Coaching is like teaching in some ways. I work with children in both jobs. I am teaching rules in both jobs. The jobs are different in that teams are smaller than classes. Also my team is all girls. My class has girls and boys.

Teaching Health Rules

"I teach health rules. I tell the girls they need rest and good food. If we play on a hot day, the girls must drink juice or water during the game. If it is too hot, we shouldn't play. The health of the girls is important.

Teaching Safety Rules

"I also teach the girls important safety rules. Bat safety is one of the first things the girls learn. The girls shouldn't throw bats. The girls put the bats down before they run. Also, the girls have to have clothes over their legs. I teach them about the clothes, so if they fall getting on base, they shouldn't get hurt."

Teaching the Game

The girls learn to bat. They learn how to catch and throw. They learn how to run the bases and to always watch the coach for directions.

Training Good Sports

"Above all else, I teach them that winning is not important. For myself, being a **good sport** is what the game is really all about," she says. A good sport is someone who behaves in a fair and helpful way.

"I want the girls to know they shouldn't say anything bad at a game. I tell them to make up their minds always to find something good to say. I want them to know that's important. They'll shout 'Nice cut!' 'Good eye!' or 'Good Swing!' even if the ball is not hit. They play the best they can. They play as a team. They enjoy softball."

Meet Eldon Muller

"How are the vegetables today?" Eldon Muller asked. He is with other workers in one of the large rooms set up as a farm.

"The vegetables are larger and more healthy-looking every day," another worker answered.

Eldon Muller looked at the computers. Everything was just right.

Eldon Muller—Farmer for the Future

"All the people of the world are neighbors," Eldon Muller says. "My job is to try to find new and different food to feed the people of the future all over the world."

Space Farms for the Future

"The farm where I lived as a boy is very different from the farms here at work. Here we try new kinds of farming. In the future, we will be farming in space. We will use computers. We may even have robot farmers doing some of the work," Eldon Muller explained. "Farms of today and farms of the future are alike in some ways too. Farms grow food to eat. Farms need people to work.

"I feel certain that computers will do most of the farming in space. They'll be used to see if the plants in space are healthy. They will see that the plants do not get too hot or too cold. What else? They'll turn the lights on and off above the plants in space."

Learning About Food for the Future

"You know what you eat today. You know the healthy foods. You know what food has the most protein. You know what flavors you like best," Mr. Muller says. "But what will people eat many years from today? How will they grow food? What flavors will they want? It is my job to find out.

"One thing is certain about the future. We must make up our minds today to make what we have last for the future."

A New Food for the Future

Eldon Muller works with vegetables and grains from all over the world. He works with wheat, corn, rice, and the winged bean. The **winged bean** is a vegetable that has more protein than almost any other vegetable. **Protein** is a food part the body needs. Protein helps the body grow and stay healthy. Mr. Muller feels almost certain the winged bean will be used in the future. He is certain the winged bean will be used to feed people the protein they need.

Finding New Ways

"Much of earth is sand and **salt water.**
The sea is a large body of salt water," Mr.
Muller says. "If we can grow food in sand,
use salt water to feed plants, or grow
plants in air without earth, it is certain
to help feed people in the future."

So Mr. Muller and others try ways to
grow vegetables in sand. They try to grow
plants in salt water. They are trying to
find ways to save water by using the same
water for the plants over and over again.

Mr. Muller and others are trying to figure out how vegetables high in protein and with good flavor can grow in space. They are also trying to make loads of fish grow faster.

One thing that's certain is that people like Mary Ellen MacAndrews and Eldon Muller and the people he works with are good neighbors. They care about other people.

Meet a Reader

Jeff, a second-grader from Georgia, loves to visit the library. He is very proud to have his own library card.

Jeff picks a book to read because it looks "real good." Jeff explains that he looks at the name of the book, its photos or pictures, and what it is about.

When Jeff hears the word *neighbor,* he thinks of feeding a friend's pet, talking to his friends on the bus, or just talking over a fence about things that are happening.

Comprehension Check

Think and Discuss

1. Why would Mary Ellen MacAndrews and Eldon Muller make good neighbors?
2. How are teaching and coaching alike?
3. Name two ways farms of today are like the farms we may have in the future.
4. Name two ways the farms of today are different from farms of the future.
5. Would you like a job like Eldon Muller's? Why or why not?

Comprehension: Comparisons

Communication Workshop

Talk

Mary Ellen and Eldon are alike in some ways. They are different in other ways. Talk with a friend. Name three ways they are alike and three ways they are different.

Speaking/Listening: Discussion

Write

List the ways Mary Ellen and Eldon are alike and different. Read your list to your friend.

Writing Fluency: List

172

LOOKING BACK

See your
Thinker's
Handbook
for tips.

Prewriting

Thinking and Writing About the Section
You have read about neighbors. You can write a paragraph to tell your family about them. First, copy and finish the sentences.

• We read three stories about neighbors.
• In "A Visit to Green Street," we read about
_____ .
• In "Rabbit's New Neighbor," we read about Rabbit who thought her neighbor was an elephant because _____ .
• In "Two Good Neighbors," we read about two neighbors, _____ and _____ .

Writing

Write the first sentence, the main idea, and your completed sentences in paragraph form. Use your Writer's Handbook if you need help.

Revising

Did you start the first word a few spaces from the left? Do all of your sentences follow each other? Make changes, proofread, and write a clean copy.

Presenting

Read your paragraph to your family.

5

Being Afraid

Cats are afraid of elephants. Elephants are afraid of mice. Of what are mice afraid?

Are you afraid of anything? People can be afraid of things. People can be afraid of the dark. People can be afraid of big animals.

Read about what some people and animals are afraid of and what they do about being afraid.

Using Connecting Words

Bill said, "You may have a peach <u>and</u> an apple."

Joan said, "You may have a peach <u>or</u> an apple."

Mike said, "You may have a peach, <u>but</u> not an apple."

How many pieces of fruit did Bill say you may have? Bill used the word *and*. Here Bill means you may have two pieces of fruit.

How many pieces of fruit did Joan say you may have? Joan used the word *or*. Here Joan means you may have one piece of fruit.

Words such as *and, or,* and *but* bring ideas together. These words are important to understanding what you read.

Read about Bill and Joan. Find the words that bring ideas together.

Some people are afraid of insects and snakes. Joan is not afraid of spiders or snakes, but Joan is afraid of bees. Bill is afraid of spiders. He is afraid of ants.

1. Some people are afraid of insects. What else is true about some people?

The word *and* in the first sentence helps us understand that some people are afraid of insects *and* snakes.

2. Which is true about Joan?
   a. Joan is afraid of spiders.
   b. Joan is not afraid of snakes.

The word *or* helps us understand that Joan is not afraid of snakes.

3. What else is true about Joan?
   a. Joan is afraid of bees.
   b. Joan is not afraid of bees.
4. Change the last two sentences of the paragraph into one sentence that tells what Bill is afraid of. Use *and, or,* or *but*.

Practicing Connecting Words

Read about Tina's class and find the words that bring ideas together.

Tina's class has a frog and a snake. Bob is afraid to hold the snake but not the frog. Rosa is not afraid to hold the frog or the snake. The frog is in a bowl. The snake is in a glass cage.

1. Tina's class has a frog. What else is true about Tina's class?
2. Finish the sentence. Bob is afraid to hold the snake, but he will hold ___.
3. What is true about Rosa?
   a. Rosa is afraid to hold the snake.
   b. Rosa is not afraid to hold the snake.
4. Change the last two sentences into one sentence by using *and*, *or*, or *but*.

Tips for Reading on Your Own

- As you read "Alligator Under the Bed," look for words such as *and*, *or*, and *but* that bring ideas together.
- Use them to help you understand what you read.

The Alligator Under the Bed

adapted from a story
by Joan Lowery Nixon

"Mama!" Jill called. "Mama, come here!"
Her mother hurried into her bedroom.

"What's wrong? It's past your bedtime,"
she said. "You should be asleep."

Jill peeked out from beneath her blanket.
"There's a big gray alligator under my bed,"
she whispered.

"Now, Jill," said her mother. "I think it's
plain that you just had a bad dream. Go to
sleep, dear." She walked out of the
bedroom.

Jill could hear the alligator's teeth
click, click, clicking together.

Jill was really frightened.

"Dad!" she called. "Dad, I need you!"

Dad was there in a minute! "What's the matter? Why aren't you asleep?" he asked.

Jill hid beneath her blanket. "I'm not asleep because there's a big gray alligator hiding under my bed!" she whispered.

Dad said, "It should be plain that an alligator couldn't get under your bed. Don't imagine things, Jill!"

He gave Jill a kiss and a moment later left the bedroom.

Suddenly Jill heard the alligator's teeth making an awful clicking sound. She was even more frightened than before. It was plain she was not dreaming. She would never dream about alligators.

Jill was quiet as long as she could be. Then she shouted, "Help! I'm frightened! There's a big gray alligator under my bed!"

Uncle Harry peeked in. "I heard clicking noises coming from this room," he said.

Jill peeked out from beneath the blanket. "It's the alligator," she whispered.

Uncle Harry folded his arms and sat down to chat. "So that's where he is," he said.

"Who?" Jill asked.

"The alligator. His name is George, isn't it?" said Uncle Harry.

"No, his name is Alberta," Jill said.

Uncle Harry grinned. "Well, I never was any good at remembering names," he said. "But I believe it's the same alligator."

"Why is he under my bed?" Jill asked.

"He's probably comfortable there. He feels warm as toast," Uncle Harry said. "He thinks it's a good hiding place. It's a good thing you found him."

"Why?" Jill whispered as she came out from beneath the blanket.

"Well," Uncle Harry explained, "when people have lost something special like an alligator, I imagine they want him back."

Jill sat up. "Who lost him?" she asked.

"His family," said Uncle Harry. "Isn't it sad that he's here, hiding under your bed, when he should really be home enjoying reading bedtime stories to his children?"

Jill thought a moment. "We better tell him to go home," she said.

"That's a good idea." Uncle Harry grinned. "You tell him. It's your bed he's under."

Jill peeked beneath her bed. It was very dark and very hard to see the alligator.

"Go home, Alberta!" she shouted. "It's bedtime. Your family wants to hear a bedtime story. They want you home right this minute!"

She sat up and looked at Uncle Harry. "He's comfortable and wants to stay under the bed," she said.

"The problem with alligators," he explained, "is that they don't like you to know they can't do something. Alberta is too proud to tell you that he doesn't know how to open the front door."

"You could do it for him," Jill said.

"Good idea," Uncle Harry said. He walked to the bedroom door. "Come with me, Alberta."

"Wait," Jill said. "He can't go with you, because he's a big alligator, and he's stuck beneath the bed."

"Right! I should have thought of that," Uncle Harry said.

Uncle Harry folded back the blanket, reached under the bed, and began to tug and groan, tug and groan.

"What are you doing?" Jill asked.

"I'm pulling him out." Uncle Harry groaned. Suddenly he fell back. "He's not stuck now!" said Uncle Harry.

"You got him out?" Jill asked.

"Right," Uncle Harry said. "And now he's going back to his family. They must miss him. Why don't you stand by the door and watch Alberta follow me to the front door?"

Uncle Harry snapped his fingers and walked to the front door. Jill jumped out of bed and hurried after him. She heard the front door open and her father ask, "What are you doing?"

"I'm sending the alligator home," Uncle Harry explained, snapping his fingers. Then suddenly his voice changed, and he sounded a little angry.

"Good-by, Alberta," he said. "Don't come back and try any tricks again!"

The front door shut.

Jill heard her father laugh and say, "Harry, you and Jill are two of a kind."

Jill ran back into her bedroom and jumped into bed. In a few minutes, she saw Uncle Harry peeking into her room.

"Uncle Harry," she asked, "what did Dad mean when he said we were two of a kind?"

"Maybe he thinks we look just alike," Uncle Harry said.

Jill looked at Uncle Harry. He was round and fat. She giggled a little.

Jill thought for a moment. Then suddenly she knew the answer.

"I know!" she said, feeling very proud of herself. "Dad thinks we are two of a kind, because we knew what to do about Alberta."

"I think you are right," Uncle Harry said, smiling. "I think you are right."

He folded Jill's blanket so she would be comfortable and warm as toast. Then he whispered, "Good night."

Soon Jill was fast asleep.

Meet the Author

"I wrote stories when I was a child," Joan Lowery Nixon remembers. "My mother and father helped me by building a theater for puppets. I wrote stories, and then we put on shows for schools and groups.

"Now as a writer of books for children, I try to remember what it was like when I was a child. I try to understand how a child would feel today. I hope that some of the children who read my books will say, 'Yes, I feel that way too. I liked reading that book.'"

Joan Lowery Nixon writes about places or people she knows. Two of her children asked her to write stories for them. "And put us in it!" they said. That is how *The Mystery of Hurricane Castle* was written.

Joan Lowery Nixon was a schoolteacher in California before she began to write. Now she writes all the time.

She won an award for best children's book with *The Alligator Under the Bed*. She has also written *The Mysterious Red Tape Gang* and *The Secret Box Mystery*.

Comprehension Check

See your Thinker's Handbook for tips.

Think and Discuss

1. Did Jill really believe there was an alligator under her bed? Why or why not?
2. What did Uncle Harry do to help Jill?
3. How would you have gotten rid of Alberta?
● 4. Finish the sentence. Jill said she saw an alligator, but Uncle Harry ___.
● 5. Turn to page 183. Change the first two sentences into one sentence by using *and*, *or*, or *but* without changing the meaning.

● Comprehension: Connecting words

Communication Workshop

Talk

The writer of the story wants you to understand how afraid Jill feels. Work with two friends. Find words the writer uses to help you understand Jill's feelings.

Speaking/Listening: Cooperative learning

Write

List the words the writer uses to tell you how Jill feels. Add your own words to the list. Read your list to the class.

Writing Fluency: List

A Bell for the Cat

A fable by Aesop
retold by Nancy Ross Ryan

Once upon a time in a castle far away,
King Mouse called a meeting of all the mice
to discuss an important problem.
  "Welcome, my brave mice," said King
Mouse.
  "Oh, oh!" whispered Shy Mouse. "He
called us brave. I'm not brave. I'm afraid."
  "You are always afraid," said Grumpy
Mouse.
  "Well, I'm not afraid. I'm just a tiny
bit frightened," said Silly Mouse.

"Not one of us is safe," said Wise Mouse. "We are all afraid. Now quiet down and let King Mouse speak."

King Mouse began, "I have called you all together to discuss our safety."

"Yes, we must figure something out," the mice whispered among themselves.

"Consider this," said King Mouse. "We live in a beautiful castle. We have warm, large rooms. The people of the castle eat well and leave food on the table for us to eat. Instead of the joy of being well fed, we are in danger. We go hungry."

"It's true," all the mice whispered.

"What can we do?" they questioned.

King Mouse pounded the table. "Order! Order! We must solve the problem of our enemy, Cat."

Zap! As soon as King Mouse said *Cat*, it bounded into the room. Its eyes were green and scary! Its mouth was angry and scary! Its teeth were white and scary!

"Here I am!" grinned Cat. Its tail waved from side to side. "The enemy you need to consider is here. What should we discuss, my pretty little mice?" Cat questioned.

"Should we discuss my green, scary eyes?
Should we discuss my big, white teeth? No,
instead, let's consider how hungry I am!"

Suddenly there were no mice to consider
anything. They had bounded off in every
direction to hide beneath anything around.

The mice hid for a long time. Finally,
when it was safe, King Mouse gave the
signal to the others. "All is clear!"

"Wow!" said Silly Mouse. "I feel as if I have seen a ghost!"

"Ghosts are not real. Ghosts are not our trouble. Cat is our problem," said Wise Mouse.

"I have an idea that may solve our problem," said Prince Mouse. "It will foil our enemy and end our trouble for good."

"Wow!" the mice shouted with joy. "Hear, hear! What will foil our enemy?"

"The trouble with Cat," began Prince
Mouse, "is that we can never hear it coming.
It is quick and quiet."

"It's true! It's true!" all the mice
whispered among themselves.

"Cat has a collar," said the prince. "The
princess of the castle put the collar on
Cat's neck to make Cat look pretty. Now, if
we put a bell on the collar, we will hear
the bell. It will be our danger signal."

"Wow!" all the mice shouted with joy.
"That's a perfect plan."

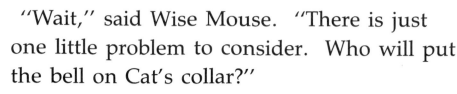

"Wait," said Wise Mouse. "There is just
one little problem to consider. Who will put
the bell on Cat's collar?"

"Not I," said Shy Mouse.

"Oh me, oh my, not I," said Silly Mouse.

"I consider it a silly plan. I will not
put a bell on Cat's collar," Grumpy said.

"Not I," said all the other mice.

"Come to order! It is a good plan. The
bell is a good danger signal," said King
Mouse. "I order someone to try."

"Wait," Prince Mouse said. "No need to order someone. It was my idea. I will do it."

"Wow!" all the mice shouted with joy.

"I'll wait until Cat is asleep," said Prince Mouse. "When I give the signal, Cat will be wearing the bell. We will be safe."

Prince Mouse watched Cat. He waited and waited. At last Cat closed its scary green eyes. Prince Mouse crawled out from behind a table, pulling the bell with him. He was frightened. It was scary to be that close to Cat! He was afraid to move, but more frightened to stand still.

Cat's scary green eyes opened wide.
Suddenly Cat jumped.

Prince ran behind a table leg just
in time. In his hurry, he left the bell
behind.

"Oh me, oh my," said Silly Mouse. "Our
plan is foiled."

"We wanted to foil Cat, and we were
foiled instead," said Shy Mouse.

"That's true," whispered the mice.

"I have a plan," said Wise Mouse.

"My plan to solve our problem," said Wise Mouse, "is to wait and watch."

"Is that a silly plan or a wise plan?" questioned Silly Mouse.

Some mice whispered, "Silly plan."

Some mice whispered, "Wise plan."

"Order, come to order," shouted King Mouse.

All the mice watched and waited. They waited and watched. Then as they watched, Cat began to play with the bell. Cat bounded after the bell around the castle floor.

Soon the princess of the castle walked by. "You found a pretty golden bell. Won't that look nice on your collar? Here, let me put it on for you."

The princess put the bell on Cat's collar. The mice lived happily ever after.

Comprehension Check

Think and Discuss

1. Why do the mice want to put a bell on Cat?
2. Why won't most mice put a bell on Cat?
3. Do you think putting a bell on Cat is a good idea? Why or why not?
- 4. Which details in the story help you picture where the mice live?
- 5. Which details help you picture Cat?

● Comprehension: Details

Communication Workshop

Talk

In the way Aesop told this story, no mouse is brave enough to put a bell on the cat. The story ends with the cat not having a bell. Ask your class which ending they like better. Why?

Speaking/Listening: Class discussion

Write

Write the ending you like better, or make up a new ending. Read your story ending to your class.

Writing Fluency: Story ending

203

To be read by the teacher

Night Sounds

by John Travers Moore

Slow and quiet the night descends.
Do you hear something?

Are we alone or have we friends—
Do you hear something?

It's not the stir that bothers quite
As much as silence in the night—
Do you hear something?

Some Things Frighten Me

by Rae W. Lyons

Hi. My name is Peggy. I'm seven and a half years old. I can do almost anything by myself. Most of the time I'm brave too. At least I think I am.

I'm not afraid of storms in the night. If I hear sharp, loud noises in the dark, I don't feel I'm in danger. I just curl up in bed and don't let the noises scare me. Sometimes I let Joy, my cat, curl up in bed with me. The loud, sharp noises may frighten Joy, but at least when she is curled up with me, she's not afraid.

Once, when I was sitting on the porch, a big spider crawled up next to me. I didn't race off the porch. I brushed the spider off the porch. I was really brave.

Did you ever reach into a bag for a piece of cord and have something crawl on your hand? I did! Would you be scared? Would you let go of the cord? Would you take a chance and take the cord out of the bag to see what it was? I wasn't scared. At least I don't remember that I was scared. I took a chance and took out the cord. Guess what? It was a silly little ant!

Some things do frighten me. Once in awhile, but not often, I'm afraid.

I took swimming lessons for the first time this summer. On the first day, I was afraid to go into the water. I just waited and watched. The water looked awfully deep.

Judi, my very best friend, was already in the water. She was having a great time. "Peggy," she called. "Here I am! Come on in! What's the matter? Are you scared?"

I didn't say anything. I was afraid all right. The water was deep. Perhaps it was cold too. I really didn't want to go in.

I made myself get in the water.
It wasn't so bad once I got used to it, but
I stayed by the side for a long time.

At the next lesson, I learned to float.
It was hard at first. I was really scared
when I went under the water, but my teacher
talked to me in a gentle but firm voice. She
held me with a firm hand and showed me how
to float. She held me until I could float by
myself.

It wasn't long before I could swim by
myself. I am not afraid of the water now.
Perhaps I was frightened because I had never
been swimming before. Sometimes it scares me
to do new things. I can't help it.

Another thing that scared me is ghosts. Once Judi and I went to the library. We got this old book about ghosts. The pictures were scary! There was a picture of a ghost that looked mean and ugly. The ghost wore an ugly costume and had giant sharp teeth. It had a big ugly mark over one eye.

That night I curled up and read the book late into the night. Then I fell asleep.

Did you ever get really scared by a dream? Well, I was scared that night. In my dream, a ghost came to take me away. It wore the same dark, scary costume as the ghost in the book. It had a scary grin. In my dream, I tried to get away, but I couldn't run fast enough.

Suddenly I heard a sharp, loud noise. I sat up in bed to see what it was. The book about ghosts had fallen on the floor!

I know there are no such things as real ghosts. They are only in books and on TV.

I'm not the only one who gets scared.
Judi does sometimes too. Judi is afraid of
big dogs. She sees the sharp teeth or hears
them bark and wants to run away.

This kind of fear can be helpful. It can
tell Judi that she may be in danger. A fear
of real danger helps you remember to be
careful. Even a dog who does not look angry
may not understand that you want to play. It
may snap.

Judi waits until she is invited by the
dog's owner to come closer. Then if the
dog's owner has a firm hold of the dog, she
will pet it. Perhaps one day Judi will learn
not to fear dogs.

Different things scare different people.
My friend Fern is shy. She's afraid to talk
to people. One time my friends and I were
all at the park playing a game. Fern was in
the park too. She watched from a long way
off. She would not come play with us.

After awhile, she came a little bit
closer. She looked to see what we were
playing.

I called, "Do you want to play, Fern?"

Fern said yes. That's the way Fern is.
You have to invite her to play with you.

Are you shy? One way to get over being shy is to set a goal to make a friend. Take a chance and invite someone to play after school. Perhaps you will make a new friend.

People who have fears are alike because they feel they are in danger. They are different because they are afraid of different things. They behave in a different way when they are frightened.

Perhaps when people understand why they are afraid, they won't be frightened any longer. My mother says now that I've talked about ghosts, dark shadows, and deep water, chances are I won't be frightened of these things any longer.

Think and Discuss

1. Name three things that frighten people in "Some Things Frighten Me."
2. How can fear be helpful?
• 3. You reach into a bag. Something in there crawls on your hand. Where is the thing that crawls on your hand?
• 4. Judi is in the water. "Here I am!" she calls. Where is Judi?
• 5. I made myself get into the water. It wasn't so bad. What wasn't so bad?

● Comprehension: Referents

Communication Workshop

Talk

Fern is shy. Talk with a group of your friends. What can friends do to help people like Fern get over being shy?

Speaking/Listening: Group discussion

Write

Write a paragraph about how to help someone who is shy. Read your paragraph to the class.

Writing Fluency: Paragraph

LOOKING BACK

Thinking and Writing About the Section

See your
Thinker's
Handbook
for tips.

Prewriting

You have read about being afraid. You can write a paragraph to tell a friend things people and animals are afraid of. First, finish these sentences on your own paper.

- People and animals are afraid of many things.
- Mice are afraid of _____.
- Some children might be afraid of _____ under their beds.
- Other children might be afraid of _____ or _____.

Writing

Write the main idea (the first sentence above) and your finished sentences in paragraph form. Use your Writer's Handbook if you need help.

Revising

Did you start the first word a few spaces from the left? Do all of your sentences follow each other? Make changes, proofread, and write a clean copy.

Presenting

Read your paragraph to a friend.

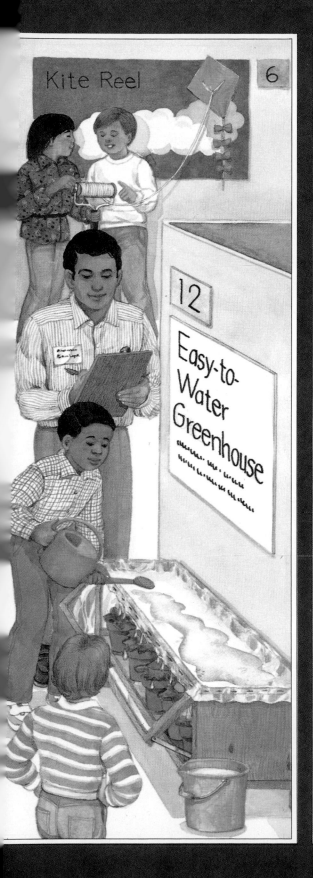

6

That's Clever!

Being clever can mean thinking of new ways to do things. People can draw clever pictures or make and say clever things.

Look at the picture. What are the children doing? What clever things do you see?

In the next stories, you will read about people and animals. See if you can figure out how each one is clever!

Drawing Conclusions

Can you tell what Karen, Linda, and Bill are doing? How does each child feel? What clues in the picture help you to know?

There are no words to help you know that the children are watching something scary. You have to look at the picture and figure things out on your own. In stories, some things are not always said in words. Just as you found clues in the picture, you have to figure things out in a story by looking for clues as you read. Finding the right clues will help you figure things out on your own.

Read the story. Look for clues that tell you what time of year the story takes place.

One cold and windy morning, John looked out his bedroom window. The ground was white. John saw his friends sliding down hills and making snow figures.

John ran down the stairs with a big smile on his face. He put on his coat and hat. He also put on his mittens. Then he ran outside to join his friends!

1. What time of year does this story take place?
2. What clues in the story help you to know?

The story takes place in winter. The clues that help you are that it is cold and windy, the ground is white, and children are outside making snow figures and sliding down hills.

3. How does John feel about the snow? How do you know?
4. Why does John need to put on so many clothes?

Practicing Drawing Conclusions

Read the story below. Look for clues that tell you who or what is telling the story.

Every day, I wait for Suzy to come to school. During school, I can hear the teacher talking. It's time for writing! Suzy uses me to write her name on the paper. Then, as Suzy pushes me across the paper, one of the words appears. Oh oh! She is writing it wrong. She turns me over so I can make the mistake go away. Then she tries again. When school is over, she puts me away until the next day.

1. Who or what is telling this story?
2. What clues in the story helped you figure it out?

Tips for Reading on Your Own

- Remember that in some stories, things are not always said in words.
- As you read the next story, look for clues that will help you figure things out on your own.

The Wise Clown

by Paul Galdone

based on a tale by Francois Rabelais

There is an old saying that a wise man can hear clever words from a clown.

This story happened long ago in a small town far away.

Many years ago, a hungry porter stopped in front of the shop of a roast meat seller. A fat goose was roasting over a fire. The goose smelled so good that it made the porter even hungrier.

The porter took a small loaf of bread from the pack he was wearing. The bread was to be his meal. Before each bite he held the bread up to be flavored by the smoke from the roasting goose.

From behind the table the cook watched, but said nothing.

The porter was taking the last bite. The cook suddenly took him by the neck and told the porter to pay him for the smoke of the roast goose.

"But," said the porter, "you have sold nothing. I have taken nothing of yours. I should pay you nothing. As for the smoke, it would have gone into the air if I was standing here or not. Who has ever heard of selling smoke?"

Then the cook shouted in a loud voice, "I
have never seen you before now. I don't see
why I should feed you with the smoke of my
good roast goose. If you do not pay me at
once I will take the wood from your pack.
Then I will split the wood and use it for my
kitchen fires."

The cook started to pull at the strap on
the bulky pack the porter was wearing. The
strong porter pulled himself away from the
cook's hands.

The words grew hotter. From all sides, people came running to watch what was happening.

Standing in the middle of the crowd was John the Lively. He was the King's clown.

When the cook saw him, he stopped. Then he said to the porter, "This is John the Lively. Everyone knows him as the King's clever clown. Will you let him be the judge in this fight and accept his decision?"

"Yes, I'll accept his decision!" said the porter, as he scratched his head.

John the Lively decided to help the two
men with their problem. He listened carefully
to them as they told him why they were
fighting.

Then he said in a loud voice, "Porter,
take a piece of money from your belt, if you
have it."

The porter, bowing to such a wise judge,
took a silver coin from the belt he was
wearing. Then he gave the silver coin to
John the Lively.

John the Lively accepted the silver coin
and put it in his hand. He made the coin ring
to find out if it was made of good silver.
Then he lifted it to his right eye to see if
it was well marked.

The crowd watched while the cook and the
porter waited for the decision.

Finally, John the Lively handed the coin to the porter. Then he said, "Now, make this silver coin ring on the table."

The porter dropped the silver coin on the table so everyone could hear it ring. Then he picked up the coin, and turned to John to hear his decision.

John the Lively coughed two or three times to clear his throat. Then, in a loud voice he said these words to the crowd:

"I have decided that the porter who ate his bread with the <u>smoke</u> of the goose has fully paid the cook with the <u>sound</u> of his money."

This decision by John the Lively seemed so grand and clever to the people. They thought a more clever decision could not have been made by the best judge in the world.

Comprehension Check

See your Thinker's Handbook for tips.

Think and Discuss

1. Why do the cook and the porter ask John the Lively for his help?
2. How does John solve the problem? Find the sentence that tells you his decision.
- 3. Would you call his decision a fair one? Why or why not?
- 4. How do you think the porter feels when he hears the decision? How do you know?
5. If you were John the Lively, what other ways could you have solved the problem?

- Comprehension: Drawing conclusions

Communication Workshop

Talk

Talk with a friend. Look at the pictures of the crowd. What do you think the people are saying and thinking?

Speaking/Listening: Discussion

Write

Imagine that you were part of the crowd. Write a letter to a friend telling what you saw. Give the letter to your friend.

Writing Fluency: Friendly letter

How Clever Can You Be?

You have read about clever people. Now it's your turn! See how clever you can be in finding answers to these questions.

1. What has ears but can't hear?

2. What are two things you can't eat for breakfast?

3. What has an eye, but can't see?

4. Who always goes to bed with shoes on?

5. What belongs to you, but is used more by others?

6. What time is it when an elephant sits on a fence?

See if you can make one up on your own!

Answers: 1. Corn, 2. Lunch and dinner, 3. A needle, 4. A horse, 5. Your name, 6. Time to get a new fence.

Understanding Contractions

Today is the big race! Each boy and girl worked hard to make a boat. Look at the word on each boat. Each word was made from two words you already know. Can you read all the words?

The words you already know were put together to make a shorter word called a **contraction**. In a contraction, an **apostrophe** is put in place of the letters that are left out. The apostrophe has no sound. It is there to show you that some letters were left out.

Read each word below. Remember that a contraction is made from two words you may already know.

we're   I'm   they've

What two words were put together to make each contraction? <u>We're</u> was made by putting <u>we</u> and <u>are</u> together. <u>I'm</u> was made by putting <u>I</u> and <u>am</u> together. <u>They've</u> was made by putting <u>they</u> and <u>have</u> together.

Practicing Contractions

Name the two words that were put together to make each underlined contraction.

"<u>I'm</u> excited about the race!" Jim said to Kathy. "<u>You've</u> been in the race before. Do you think <u>you're</u> going to race again?"

Tips for Reading on Your Own

- When you see a word with an apostrophe, it might be a contraction made from two words.
- Knowing the two words will help you understand what the contraction means.

Navajo Pet

by Patricia Miles Martin

Luke Big Moose was a Navajo Indian. He lived in a house on the plains of Wyoming.

Luke had a pet goat. Every morning the goat watched while Luke climbed into a big yellow bus that stopped near his house. Luke rode a mile down the road to school. The goat watched the bus until it was out of sight.

Danny Long John was also a Navajo Indian who lived on the plains of Wyoming. He had a pet too. He had an old horse.

Luke liked everything about Wyoming except Danny and his horse.

In school the one who behaved best was asked to carry out all the old papers. The papers had to be put in a deep hole behind the schoolhouse.

Luke pushed Danny Long John at least once a day so Luke never got to carry the papers out. Sometimes Danny carried them.

While Luke and Danny were in school, Danny's horse and Luke's goat went everywhere together. Sometimes they went to the school. Most of the time they went far away, over the flatland to the red-brown bluffs.

But in the afternoon, when Luke came home from school, his goat was always in front of the house waiting for him. Some days Danny's horse was there too.

One afternoon Danny came to Luke's house. He was holding a rope.

"Why do you keep my horse?" he asked.

"Why does he follow my goat?" Luke asked.

Danny pushed the goat, and the goat butted him.

"That goat knows who his enemies are," Luke said. "That's more than your old horse knows."

Danny put his rope around the horse's neck. He jumped up on its back and trotted away.

The next morning, Luke sat by his house playing with the goat. By and by, the horse trotted into sight again, and ran up to them. Fast as he could, Danny dashed over too.

"You've got my horse again," he shouted.

"Keep your horse away from my goat," Luke said.

On Sunday morning Luke went outside
to the sheep pen and opened the gate. Luke
and the goat took the sheep through
the gate. They were looking for a patch of
green where the sheep might feed.

They passed Danny's house. Danny's old
horse was tied to a pole beside the door.

Near the bluffs Luke found a place, and
there they stopped. The sheep nibbled on
wild grasses. The goat ate too.

In the middle of the morning, Luke heard a
neighing sound. He looked around. There
was Danny's horse, its rope hanging behind.

The horse ate with the goat and the sheep.

On the way home that night, Luke passed Danny's house again. Danny was not in sight. Luke walked the horse to Danny's door. He tied the rope to the wooden pole beside the house and left the horse there.

Luke and the goat hurried on with the sheep.

On Monday afternoon when Luke came home from school, his goat was not waiting at the house.

"My goat is gone," Luke said to his grandpa. "I have looked everywhere. I think Danny Long John took it."

"Get the goat back," his grandpa said.

Luke started out for Danny's house. He ran through a field of corn and a patch of wild flowers. He stopped in front of a small gray house and called for Danny.

"Danny, my goat is gone. I came to get it," he called.

Danny's mother answered. "Danny's horse is gone," she said. "Danny has gone to your house to get his horse."

Luke started running home, but then saw Danny running toward him. Danny was carrying a rope.

"You've taken my goat," Luke said.

"You've taken my horse," Danny said.

The two boys were ready to fight when a horse neighed.

"That neighing sounds like my horse," Danny said.

Then they heard a goat.

"That sounds like my goat," Luke said.

What do you think has happened to the animals?

The sounds came from far away. The boys ran toward the sounds. They stopped to listen, and then ran toward the schoolhouse as fast as they could. Behind the schoolhouse, the horse was standing and waiting.

"The goat is down in the hole," Danny said.

Slowly, Luke went down into the hole, and tied Danny's rope around the goat's middle. Together, the two boys pulled the goat up.

Do you think Danny and Luke will become friends? Why or why not?

Danny untied the rope on the goat, and the goat butted him.

"That goat doesn't know who its friends are," Danny said.

"You're right," Luke said.

Danny put his rope around the horse's neck and jumped up on its back.

"Get up behind me, Luke," Danny said. "We'll all go home together."

Luke jumped up. The goat walked beside them. The boys rode along, past the field of corn and the patch of wild flowers.

"If we stick together, we'll always know where our pets are," Danny said.

"You're right," said Luke. "From now on, we'll stick close together."

Now at school the teacher lets Luke and Danny carry out the papers. And after school Luke and Danny ride around on the horse together. The goat goes, too.

Sometimes they go across the flatland to the red-brown bluffs. Most of the time, they go everywhere the goat wants to go.

Meet the Author

"The Navajo Pet" was written by Patricia Miles Martin. Since she was very young, she has enjoyed learning and writing about Indians.

Patricia Miles Martin remembers the first story she wrote. When she was seven years old, her family lived on a farm. One day as she sat in the old barn, she listened to the rain as it hit the roof. At that moment, she wrote her first story about the things she saw, smelled, and heard.

She has written *Annie and the Old One, Rabbit Garden, Mississippi Possum,* and many other stories. Sometimes Ms. Martin uses the name Miska Miles for her books. When you're looking for her books, look for both names!

Comprehension Check

- 1. Do Luke and Danny become friends? What clues in the story help you to know?
2. Are Luke and Danny friends at the beginning of the story? How do you know?
3. Why doesn't Luke get to carry the papers?
- 4. Were you right about what happened to the horse and the goat? Find the sentence that helped you with your answer.
5. Did the boys work well together while helping the goat? Why or why not?

- Comprehension: Predicting outcomes

Communication Workshop

Talk

Talk with a group about Luke and Danny. How do they act towards each other at the beginning? How do they change?

Speaking/Listening: Cooperative learning

Write

List three things Luke and Danny do by the end of the story that show they are friends. Read your list to your group.

Writing Fluency: List

Puss in Boots

by Paul Galdone
based on a tale by Charles Perrault

Once long ago there was a miller. When he
was so old that he could no longer work, he
gave all of his things to his three sons.

He left the mill to his oldest son, and
the donkey to his second son. To his youngest
son he left the cat, Puss.

The youngest son was very sad.

 "My brothers can use the mill and the
donkey to work together every month of the
year," he said. "But how can I ever make a
living with just this cat?"

Now Puss was a clever cat and could
understand what people said.

Puss said to the youngest son, "Have boots
made for me so that I can run through the
field. And get me a sack with a cord. If you
do this, you will never be unhappy again."

The miller's son was very surprised to hear the cat speak, but he did as Puss told him. He got Puss a sack with a strong cord and he had fine red boots made to the cat's size.

When Puss had learned to run in his new boots, he went to a field where many wild rabbits lived. Puss put some carrots in the sack. Then he hid behind a tree and waited.

Soon a hungry young rabbit came along and hopped right into the sack. Puss quickly pulled the cord. He put the sack on his back and hurried to the King's castle.

Puss knocked on the door. Out came the King and his men.

"How do you do, your Majesty," said Puss.
"My owner, the Marquis of Carabas, sends this
rabbit to you."

"I have never heard of the Marquis of
Carabas," said the King. "But I love rabbit,
so I will gladly accept this gift."

The next day Puss went to a wheat field.
This time, he put golden grain into the sack.
Then he hid in the high grass and made the
sound of a partridge. Two partridges heard
the call and ran into the sack.

Puss hurried to the King's castle.

"Good day, your Majesty," said Puss. "Here
is another gift from the Marquis of Carabas."

The King looked at the partridges. Then he
said, "The Marquis of Carabas must be a fine
man to send me all these fine treats."

As Puss was leaving the castle, he heard the King's coachmen talking.

"The King has said that we should get his coach ready for a ride along the river today," said one.

"And he will be taking the princess with him," said the other.

Puss ran all the way from the King's castle to the youngest son's house.

"Today your riches will be made!" Puss cried. "All you must do is go for a swim in the river. Leave the rest to me."

The miller's son did as Puss told him. He went to the river, took off his clothes, and jumped into the water. Puss hid the young man's clothes behind a rock.

No sooner had Puss done this than the King's coach pulled up.

"Help! Help!" Puss shouted as he ran into the road. "The Marquis of Carabas has been robbed!"

When the King heard this, he stuck his head out of the window.

"Stop the coach!" he ordered. He saw Puss and remembered the many fine gifts Puss's owner had given to him.

"Your Majesty, someone has taken my owner's clothes," said Puss.

"Coachmen," the King ordered, "drive back to the castle. You're to get my best clothes for the Marquis of Carabas."

The miller's son was very surprised.

"Who is the Marquis of Carabas?" he whispered to Puss.

"I have told the King that you're the Marquis," Puss whispered.

The miller's son dressed in the beautiful clothes. He looked as fine as any Marquis.

"Now you must thank the King," said Puss. "Leave the rest to me and your riches will soon be made."

The miller's son thanked the King for the new clothes.

"You're most welcome," said the King. "Would you please join us for a ride?"

The miller's son sat next to the Princess. She was happy to meet such a fine young man.

Puss ran on until he came to a field where some farmers were working.

"Farmers!" called Puss in a frightening voice. "When the King drives past and asks you who this field belongs to, you must say 'To the Marquis of Carabas.' If you don't, something awful will happen to you."

Soon the King passed by in his coach.

"Who does this field belong to?" he asked.

"To the Marquis of Carabas," answered the farmers, for they had been greatly frightened by Puss.

"You have very fine land," the King said to the miller's son.

The son saw what Puss was up to and said nothing. But he smiled at the Princess and she smiled back at him.

Puss ran as fast as his boots could carry him until he came to a great castle.

The castle belonged to a mean old Giant. The Giant owned all the lands the King had just passed by. For many years the Giant made the farmers work for him.

Puss had heard that the Giant could turn himself into many things.

"What do you want?" the Giant roared when he saw it was only a cat at the door.

"I could not pass this way," Puss said, "without meeting you." This greatly pleased the Giant, and he let Puss into the castle.

"Is it really true that you can change yourself into a lion or an elephant or anything you want?" asked Puss.

"Oh, yes, I can change into many animals," grinned the Giant.

A loud noise sounded through the castle. Then suddenly, an elephant appeared.

"Wow!" said Puss, who jumped out of the way of the swinging trunk.

Suddenly the elephant roared and a lion appeared.

"That's great!" cried Puss, though he was very much afraid of the lion. "It must be easy for you to turn into something large. But can you turn into something small?"

"Yes!" roared the lion, and in a moment a little mouse ran across the floor.

That was just what Puss had been waiting for. With one jump he caught the mouse and ate it up. And that was the end of the mean old giant.

Before long the King's coach stopped at the Giant's castle.

"Welcome to the castle of the Marquis of Carabas," Puss said with a bow.

"Does this beautiful castle belong to you, too, Marquis?" asked the King.

Puss brought them all to a grand room. A fine meal had been made for them by the cook. The cook was much happier working for Puss than for the Giant.

The King was very pleased with the fine young Marquis, his castle, and all his lands.

"You may ask the princess to marry you. You both seem to like each other so very much."

The princess said yes, and they had the wedding that very afternoon.

There was a great party that lasted long into the night. Puss, in his red boots, danced all the dances.

"Thank you for all your help," the miller's son told Puss.

The next day he had a special throne made for Puss. They all lived happily ever after.

Meet the Author

Paul Galdone is the storyteller and illustrator of "Puss in Boots." Mr. Galdone enjoys drawing new pictures for stories of long ago and wanted to tell the story of "Puss in Boots" in his own words.

Paul Galdone's love for drawing began when he was a very young boy. Since then, he has made drawings for many books.

Some other old stories he has retold and made drawings for are *The Gingerbread Boy* and *The Old Woman and Her Pig.*

LOOKING BACK

Thinking and Writing About the Section
You have read about clever people and animals. You can write a paragraph to tell someone in another class how one of them was clever. First, finish this chart on your own paper.

See your Thinker's Handbook for tips.

Story	Character	What was clever
The Wise Clown		
Navajo Pet		
Puss in Boots		

Writing Choose one character. Write a paragraph to tell what the character did that was clever. Use your Writer's Handbook if you need help.

Revising Does your paragraph begin with a sentence that tells what character was clever (the main idea)? Make changes, proofread, and write a clean copy.

Presenting Read your paragraph to someone in another class. Would he or she like to read the story?

Books to Read

Lost in the Store
by Larry Bograd

Bruno is lost in a busy store. He can't find his mother or father. What will he do?

Animals that Migrate
by Caroline Arnold

Did you know that many animals have two homes? You'll be surprised at the way they travel from one home to another.

Molly Moves Out
by Susan Pearson

Molly the rabbit doesn't like the things her brothers and sisters do. She finally decides to find a little home for her very own.

Amelia Bedelia Helps Out
by Peggy Parish

Amelia Bedelia has a long list of things to do for Miss Emma. You'll enjoy her clever ways of solving problems.

Student's Handbooks

Writer's Handbook

Thinker's Handbook

Word Study Handbook

Glossary

To be read by the teacher

This handbook answers the kinds of questions you might ask when you are writing your **Looking Back** papers. It can also help you with the other writing you do.

The handbook tells you about the four writing steps: Prewriting, Writing, Revising, and Presenting.

Prewriting

1. What is prewriting?

Prewriting is what you do to get ready to write. It is when you start to write down ideas.

To begin prewriting, you can talk over ideas with a friend, your teacher, or the boys and girls in your class.

You can also put your ideas down in a list or on a chart to help you get started.

2. Who will read what I write?

There are many different people who may read your work. Some people are your teacher, a friend, your family, or even someone you do not know. You can also write just for yourself.

It is important when prewriting to keep in mind who will read your work. This will help you know what words to use and what ideas to put in or to leave out. For example, if you write a letter to a friend, you would want to use the kind of words you use when you talk to him or her.

3. How can I "talk" to others when I write?

You can write sentences about something you like to share with a friend. You can write a friendly letter or an invitation to send to a friend.

4. How can I give information to others when I write?

You can write a paragraph to tell about something you have read to share with others.

Writing

1. What do I do when I begin writing?

Think about what you were asked to write and who will read it. You can also think about your big point and look at what you did in prewriting.

When you are ready to write, put down all of your ideas. Don't stop writing, even if you are not happy with all of your ideas. Don't worry about making mistakes, such as how to spell a word. Just keep writing down your ideas.

2. I have written down my ideas. What do I do next?

Stop for a few minutes. Read what you wrote. Think about your big point. Is it clear?

You can also check to see if your paper shows what you were asked to write about. Were you to write a friendly letter or an invitation? Were you to write a paragraph to tell others about what you read?

3. I wrote a friendly letter. How do I know if it is good?

A good friendly letter sounds friendly. A friendly letter has five parts: a date, a greeting, a body, a closing, and a name.

4. I wrote an invitation. How do I know if it is good?

A good invitation tells everything the people you are inviting need to know: who the invitation is for, what they are invited to, when and where they should come, and who the invitation is from.

5. I wrote a paragraph. How do I know if it is good?

A good paragraph keeps to one idea, called the *main idea*. One sentence tells the main idea. The others tell more about it. The first sentence in a paragraph starts a few spaces from the left. This is called *paragraph form*.

Revising

1. What do I do first when I revise?

First look at *what* you wrote. Ask yourself or a partner questions like these:

- Does my friendly letter have five parts?
- Does my invitation tell everything the people I am inviting need to know?
- Does my paragraph have a main idea?

2. What do I do next when I revise?

Next, look at *how* you wrote. Ask yourself or a partner questions like these:

- Did I put commas in the date, greeting, and closing of my friendly letter?
- Did I use capital letters in the date and the names in my friendly letter or invitation?
- Is my paragraph in paragraph form?
- Do all of my sentences begin with capital letters?
- Do I have a period or a question mark at the end of each sentence?
- Did I spell words correctly?

3. How do I show any changes I want to make?

You can use proofreader's marks to show the changes you want to make on your paper. They will help you remember where you need to make a change. Look at the proofreader's marks below.

Proofreader's Marks	
≡ Make a capital letter.	ℓ Take out a word.
⊙ Add a period.	⊛ Correct the spelling.
∧ Add a word or words.	

4. What do I do when I have marked the changes I need to make?

Get a new sheet of paper. Write a clean copy of your work. Remember to use your best handwriting.

Presenting

1. How can I present my work to others?

You can share your writing in many ways. Here are some suggestions.

<u>Mail It</u>   Get help addressing an envelope. Send your letter or invitation in the mail.

<u>Make a Book</u>   Put your best papers together. Draw a picture and write a title for the cover. Staple the cover and papers together. Put your book in your classroom library so others can read it.

<u>Make a Puppet</u>   Make stick puppets. Use your puppets to act out a story you have written for a group.

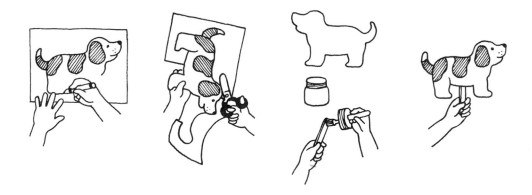

2. How can my class work together to present our work?

Your class can work together in many ways. Here are some suggestions.

Share Your Writing   Read your paper to your class. Tell them how you came up with your ideas. Explain everything you did to write the paper.

Make a Bulletin Board Display   Put all the papers your class has written up on a bulletin board. Decorate the edges of the bulletin board to show what the papers are about.

Have an Author's Day   Have everyone in your class choose their best papers. Mount the papers on cardboard. Invite parents and friends to come and read everyone's work.

To be read by the teacher

This handbook can help you with your work in *What Do I See* as well as other things you learn and do. It can help you learn by helping you think about things before, during, and after you do them. The handbook also has activities that may make you think in new ways.

Tips to Help You Think

Task 1: Understanding What You Read

To better understand what you read, think about questions like these:

- Is what I am reading making sense to me? If not, do I need to stop and reread?

- Can I figure out why the characters are acting the way they are?

- Would it help me to figure out what is happening and why, or the order in which things are happening?

- What do I need to know about what happened to tell what the story is all about?

- What important ideas do I need to know to tell what this article is all about?

Task 2: Answering Questions

To answer questions, think about *asking* yourself questions:

- Do I understand the question?

- Is this question asking for one answer or more than one answer?

- If I don't know the answer, what other questions can I ask myself that might lead me to the answer?

- What do I need to do in order to get the answer to this kind of question?

Kinds of Questions	Ways to Answer
What does this map show? Name one piece of information.	Recall, or remember, information that was *in* a story or an article.
How do the characters try to get what they want? What happens first, next, and last?	Gather and pull together several pieces of important information you read in a story or an article.
How does the character feel and how do you know? What can you tell from the information on this graph?	Use clues from what you read and use what you already know to lead you to decide something.
Why is this a good title? Do you like the story? Why?	Evaluate, or judge, what you read and give reasons or examples.

270

Task 3: Communicating Ideas

When you work with a partner or a small group, keep these questions in mind:

- Do we know what we need to do?

- Should we each take part of the work or should we work together?

- What do we need to do to get the work done—do steps in order, think of questions, or retell a story?

- Would putting our work on a chart or in a web make it clearer?

- Do we need to write a list of our ideas?

- Do we need to work for a while and then talk to each other to see how we are doing?

- Are we doing the work we were asked to do or are we talking about something else?

- Can my partner or group understand what I am saying?

- Can we put each other's ideas in our own words to be sure we understand everyone?

- Have we done what we set out to do?

Activities for You to Enjoy

Activity 1: Solving Problems

One way to solve problems is to evaluate, or judge, information. Think about questions like the following as you read the paragraph below. Then solve the problem.

- What is the problem?

- How important is it to solve the problem now?

- What are different ways I could solve the problem?

- Which is the best way to solve the problem?

Minerva Mouse always buys her food at Rhonda Raccoon's market. One day, Minerva Mouse is on her way to Rhonda's market when she trips and her money falls into a pond. The market will close soon, so she doesn't have time to go home to get more money. Although all mice can swim, Minerva is afraid of water. There is only enough food for two mice at home, but there are four mice in Minerva's family.

Think of three ways Minerva can solve her problem. What is the best way to solve it?

Activity 2: Making Decisions

One way to make decisions is to think in different ways. Think about questions like the following as you read the paragraph. Then tell what decisions you would make.

- Do I know what decisions I need to make?

- Would it help me to think of what I like or what others might like?

- Should I make a list of the different things I am deciding between?

- How much time do I have?

A store has given lots of pieces of cloth to your class. They gave you a very large piece the size of a wall, many medium-sized small pieces the size of books, and a bag of small pieces the size of peas. Think of something you could do with each size alone, and something you could do that uses all the sizes at once. Now decide—what would you do with the cloth?

Activity 3: Asking the Right Questions

One way to ask the right kind of questions is to think about *why* you need to ask them. Read the following tips and use them to help the princess ask the right kind of questions.

- Think about why you need to ask questions.

- Ask yourself what you need to know.

- Think about information you already know.

- Decide which questions will lead you to the information you need.

Dudley Dragon asked the princess if she would take care of his son, Little Drag, while he goes on a trip. The princess doesn't know much about little dragons. She needs to ask the right kind of questions so she will know what to do. Which of these questions should she ask?

What does Little Drag eat?
Does Dudley Dragon like to travel?
How can the princess reach Dudley?
When is Little Drag's bedtime?
Does Little Drag like to sing?
Does Little Drag like to spit fire?

Activity 4: Comparing Likenesses and Differences

One way to compare things is to figure out how they are alike and different. Think about questions like these as you read the paragraph. Then tell how you would help Maria.

- What do I need to find out by comparing?

- Would it help me to list what I know about each thing I am comparing?

- Should I make sure my lists are in the same order so that I can see the likenesses and differences?

- How can I decide which likenesses and differences are most important?

Rabbit, Raccoon, Squirrel, and Owl came to visit Maria. Maria wants the two who are most alike to share a room. Rabbit and Squirrel sleep all night, but Raccoon and Owl like to play at night. Rabbit and Raccoon are very quiet, but Owl and Squirrel like to talk all the time. Squirrel has a pet worm, but Owl eats worms. Help Maria figure out who should share a room.

To be read by the teacher

On the next few pages are some of the strategies you've learned to figure out the meaning and pronunciation of words.

Phonics: Consonant Sounds and Letters

Strategy 1: I can use what I know about **consonant sounds and letters** at the beginning, middle, and end of a word.

Say these words:

won	le**ss**on	be**ll**
bean	a**pp**le	**fl**ag
most	mone**y**	treat
fear	travel	gla**d**

Vocabulary and Skill Application

Write the sentences. Use the words from the box to complete the sentences.

1. I ＿＿＿ a prize for reading well.
2. My prize was a juicy red ＿＿＿.
3. It was the ＿＿＿ beautiful apple I had ever seen.
4. The reading ＿＿＿ had been fun.
5. I left when the ＿＿＿ started to ring.

Phonics: Blends and Digraphs

Strategy 2: I can use what I know about **blends and digraphs** at the beginning and end of a word.

Say these words. Listen to the sounds of the two or three letters blended together or the letters that stand for one sound at the beginning or end of each word.

plain	he**ld**	**qu**iet	sa**ng**
flute	ba**nd**	**kn**ock	pa**th**
stream	su**lk**	**sh**arp	rou**gh**
cried	lost	**wr**ong	pea**ch**

Vocabulary and Skill Application

Write the sentences. Use the words from the box to complete the sentences.

1. There was a ＿＿ at the door.
2. A boy ＿＿ a black bag in his hands.
3. There was a silver ＿＿ in the bag.
4. The boy played it and then ＿＿.
5. I was very ＿＿.
6. I asked the boy if he played in the ＿＿.
7. "Yes, but I just ＿＿ my music," he said.
8. The boy ＿＿ and said he would miss band.
9. We went to tell the teacher what was ＿＿.

Phonics: Short Vowel Sounds

Strategy 3: I can use what I know about **short vowel sounds.**

Say these words. Listen to the vowel sounds. What kind of letters are before and after the vowel in each word?

Short *a*	Short *e*	Short *i*	Short *o*	Short *u*
lap	bell	lift	knot	hug
pan	tent	thick	doll	tug
sack	send	print	shop	trunk
camp	fence	string	solve	judge

Vocabulary and Skill Application

Write the sentences. Use the words from the box to complete the sentences.

1. Mom and Dad wanted a ____ for camping.
2. They thought it would ____ their problem.
3. They didn't want to ____ me to summer

   ____ .

4. Mom, Dad, and I went to a ____ in town.
5. We bought a tent that came in a ____ bag.
6. The bag had a ____ to tie at the top.
7. Mom and Dad said it wasn't hard to ____ .
8. We put it in the ____ of the car.
9. When we got home, we gave each other a ____ .

Phonics: Long Vowel Sounds

Strategy 4: I can use what I know about **long vowel sounds.**

Say these words. Listen to the vowel sounds. Which words have two vowels together that stand for a long vowel sound? Which words have a vowel and a consonant followed by the letter *e*?

Long *a*	Long *e*	Long *o*	Long *i*	Long *u*
wait	peek	poke	size	tune
sale	dream	hope	while	rule
stay	seen	loaf	knife	tube

Vocabulary and Skill Application

Write the sentences. Use the words from the box to complete the sentences.

1. Pete heard there was a shoe ___ today.
2. On Monday he had ___ the shoes he liked.
3. Pete had taken a ___ through the window.
4. He wanted them ___ they were on sale.
5. Pete did not know his shoe ___ .
6. He also needed new ___ socks for school.
7. "I ___ Mom buys them for me," said Pete.
8. He didn't want to ___ too long.

Phonics: R-Controlled Vowels
Strategy 5: I can use what I know about
r-controlled vowels.

Say these words. Listen to the vowel sounds.
What letter comes after the vowel in each
word?

ba**r**n	he**r**	fi**r**m	po**r**ch	hu**r**t
ca**r**d	ge**r**m	sti**r**	co**r**d	cu**r**l
ma**r**k	pe**r**ch	fi**r**st	wo**r**e	tu**r**n
ya**r**d	we**r**e	shi**r**t	ho**r**se	bu**r**n

Vocabulary and Skill Application
Write the sentences. Use the words from
the box to complete the sentences.

1. Kim wanted to have a party in the ____.
2. It was her ____ to have a party.
3. She asked ____ Mom and Dad if she could.
4. This was the ____ time she had asked.
5. Kim waited on the ____ for an answer.
6. Her mom and dad ____ very understanding.
7. They didn't want to ____ her feelings.
8. They said to have it in the red ____.
9. They would move Kim's ____ out of the barn.
10. The horse had a white ____ on its nose.

Phonics: Vowel Sounds
Strategy 6: I can use what I know about **vowel sounds.**

Say these words. Listen to the vowel sounds.
What letters stand for the vowel sounds in
each word?

found	**wow**	**boy**
p**ou**nd	cr**ow**	j**oy**
b**ou**ght	cl**ow**n	c**oi**n
th**ou**ght	cr**ow**d	f**oi**l

Vocabulary and Skill Application
Write the sentences. Use the words from
the box to complete the sentences.

1. Rex saw a _____ of boys near his classroom.
2. The class was going to see a _____.
3. Rex _____ some money on the way.
4. There was a silver _____ on the floor.
5. "_____," he said.
6. Rex jumped for _____.
7. He _____ of all the things he could buy.
8. Rex was a very happy _____.
9. "What if I _____ some apples?" said Rex.
10. He thought about buying a _____ of apples.

Phonics: Endings

Strategy 7: I can use what I know about **endings.**

A. Add endings *-s, -es, -ed, -ing* without changing the root word:

　　*return　return**s**　return**ed**　return**ing***

B. Drop the *e* and add endings *-ed* or *-ing*:

　　hope + **ing** = *hop**ing***

C. Double the last consonant and add endings *-ed* or *-ing*:

　　step + p + **ed** = *step**ped** step**ping***

D. Change the *y* to *i* and add endings *-es* or *-ed*: *cry* + **ed** = *cr**ied***

Vocabulary and Skill Application

Write the words and add the endings. Complete the sentences with the words you make.

Add *-s*	Add *-es*	Add *-ed*	Add *-ing*
magnet**s**	dish**es**	return**ed**	land**ing**
pen	story	excite	chat

1. I could not find my ＿＿ to write a note.
2. They had fallen while I was ＿＿.
3. Joan told me about some new animal ＿＿.
4. I was so ＿＿ that I wanted to read them.

Structure: Syllables

Strategy 8: I can use what I know about syllabication when a word has two **syllables.**

A. When a word ends in *-le,* divide before the consonants: troub·le

B. When a word has two consonants between two vowels, divide between the two consonants: ham·mer, num·ber

C. When a word has one consonant between two vowels, divide before or after the consonant: a·corn, ped·al

---

Vocabulary and Skill Application

Write the sentences. Use the words from the list to complete the sentences.

gentle   dinner   moment   corner
uncle   wagon   final   perfect

1. Our ___ took us out.

2. We ate ___ in the park.

3. We had our ___ summer picnic together.

Structure: Prefixes

Strategy 9: I can use what I know about **prefixes.**

See also Skill Lesson: Prefixes on pages 110–111.

acorn

basket

bridge

candle

A a

a·corn   the hard seed of a special tree. See the picture. **a·corns**

an·gry   feeling or showing that you are not pleased about something: *Dad was very angry when I hit the window.*

ap·ple   A fruit that is good to eat: *Apples grow on trees.* **ap·ples**

art   drawing, painting, and other works of art: *Children in second grade learn about art.* **arts**

B b

bas·ket   a box or bowl made of dry grass or pieces of wood someone weaves together. See the picture. **bas·kets**

be·lieve   think something is true: *We believe the earth is round.* **be·lieves   be·lieved   be·liev·ing**

bridge   something put above water or land so that people or cars can cross over. See the picture. **bridg·es**

C c

can·dle   a special stick with a kind of string in it. *As the string burns, the candle gives light.* See the picture. **can·dles**

cel·e·brate   do special things on a birthday or other special day: *Each year we celebrate my birthday at Grandmother's.* **cel·e·brates   cel·e·brat·ed   cel·e·brat·ing**

chip·munk   a small, striped animal like a squirrel. See the picture. **chip·munks**

cir·cus   a show that travels from place to place: *A circus has lions and clowns.* **cir·cus·es**

com·put·er   a machine that counts or figures things out: *A computer can do work fast.* **com·put·ers**

cor·ner   place where two walls or streets meet: *He put the table in the corner of the room.* **cor·ners**

chipmunk

D d

de·cide   come to a way of thinking: *We decided to stay home.* **de·cides de·cide·ed de·cid·ing**

di·rec·tion   any way in which one may face or point: *North and south are directions.* **di·rec·tions**

dis·ap·point   to feel bad when one doesn't get what one wished or hoped for: *There was no elephant, so the circus disappointed him.* **dis·ap·points dis·ap·point·ed dis·ap·point·ing**

E e

ear·ly   in the beginning: *In his early years he learned how to brush his teeth.*

el·e·phant   the largest four-footed animal. See the picture. **el·e·phants**

e·ven   though you would not think it: *It looks dark even though it is early.*

elephant

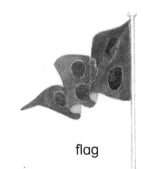

flag

garden

half

ev·er   at any time: *Does he ever sleep?*

ex·plore   go over a place and look at it: *The children explored the new playground.* **ex·plores   ex·plored   ex·plor·ing**

ex·tra   more than what is needed: *The workmen asked for extra pay.*

F f

fi·nal   coming last: *Here is the final question.*

flag   a piece of colored cloth that stands for some country or state or group. See the picture. **flags**

floor   a story of a building: *Four families live on the first floor.* **floors**

for·get   let go out of the mind: *Please don't forget to brush your teeth.* **for·gets   for·get·ting**

G g

gar·den   a piece of ground in which vegetables or flowers grow. See the picture. **gar·dens**

gen·tle   kind or friendly: *We had a gentle dog.*

H h

half   one of two parts of the same size. See the picture. **halves**

health   being well or being sick: *My mother and father care about my health.*

horse a large animal with four legs and a long tail. People ride horses. See the picture. **hors·es**

horse

I i

i·de·a a plan, picture, or thought in the mind: *Who had the idea to go the zoo?* **i·de·as**

in·vite ask someone to come to some place or to do something: *We will invite them to stay.* **in·vites in·vit·ed in·vit·ing**

J j

jam fruit cooked until it is thick: *Jam can be spread on bread or toast.* **jams**

joy a glad feeling: *She jumped for joy when she saw the circus.*

judge one who decides questions about rules: *He was a judge at the dog show.* **judg·es**

juice the part of fruit or vegetable or meat that flows like water: *The orange juice tasted sweet.* **juic·es**

K k

knife something sharp used to cut: *He cut the meat with his knife.* **knives**

knock make a noise by hitting: *Knock on the door.* **knocks knocked knock·ing**

287

lion

log

mask

L l

li·on   a large, strong, wild animal. See the picture. **li·ons**

lock   something that holds doors or windows so they cannot be opened: *The front door of most houses has a lock.* **locks**

log   a long piece from the trunk or branches of a tree. See the picture. **logs**

M m

mask   something put in front of or over the face to hide the face. See picture. **masks**

min·ute   a very small bit of time: *We should be there in a minute.* **min·utes**

mis·take   something that is not right or correct: *I made a mistake.* **mis·takes**

mo·ment   a very small space of time: *In a moment it will be dark.* **mo·ments**

mon·ey   coins and paper used to buy and sell things: *She bought some flowers with her money.*

N n

neat   clean and in order: *His room was always neat.*

nib·ble   eat away with quick, small cuts of the teeth: *The rabbit nibbled on the carrot.* **nib·bles nib·bled   nib·bling**

no·tice   to see, give thought to: *Take no notice of the dog's barking.* **no·tices   no·ticed   no·tic·ing**

O o

of·ten   many times: *It often snows in winter.*

or·der   quiet, no trouble: *Let's try to get some order in our classroom.*

P p

par·tridge   a wild bird. See the picture.

per·fect   all right or having no mistakes: *He turned in a perfect paper.*

pho·to   a picture made with a machine for taking pictures. See the picture. **pho·tos**

pic·nic   a party with a meal outside: *We had a picnic at the park.* **pic·nics**

plan·et   one of the bodies, like the earth, that moves around the sun: *The earth is a planet, but the sun is a star.* **plan·ets**

pro·tein   one of the things which animals and plants need to grow: *Milk and meat have protein.*

Q q

ques·tion   a thing asked to find out something: *A teacher asks questions.* **ques·tions**

qui·et   with little or no noise: *It was a quiet night.*

R r

re·peat   do or say again: *Please repeat that word.* **re·peats re·peat·ed   re·peat·ing**

re·ward   give something for something done: *She rewarded him for finding the lost dog.* **re·wards re·ward·ed   re·ward·ing**

roast   bake meat right over a fire: *The cook roasts a pig.* **roasts   roasted   roasting**

ro·bot   machine that follows orders to do work. See the picture. **ro·bots**

partridge

photo

robot

289

scarecrow

S s

scare·crow a figure dressed in old clothes. A scarecrow is set up in a field to frighten birds. See the picture. **scare·crows**

shad·ow the darkness made by someone or a thing in a bright light: *Sometimes my shadow is very long.* **shad·ows**

sign any mark or thing used to tell something or stand for something. See the picture. **signs**

space·ship a kind of plane used for traveling through space to other planets. See the picture. **space·ships**

stream running water: *Most streams become rivers.* **streams**

sulk be quiet because of bad feelings: *He sulks when he does not get his own way.* **sulks** **sulked** **sulk·ing**

T t

telephone

tel·e·phone something used to talk to someone far away. See the picture. **tel·e·phones**

trash stuff of no use: *That box is trash.*

true to believe something is right: *This is a true story.*

trust believe firmly in or feel safe with someone or something: *The boy trusted his friend.* **trusts** **trust·ed** **trust·ing**

U u

un·cle your father or mother's brother: *My mother's brother, John, is my uncle.* **un·cles**

wagon

un·der·stand know what something means: *Now I understand your note.* **un·der·stands un·der·stand·ing**

V v

veg·e·ta·ble a plant used for food: *Corn, peas, and beans are vegetables.* **veg·e·ta·bles**

W w

wag·on a four-wheeled box for riding in and carrying loads. See the picture. **wag·ons**

weath·er vane a thing to show which way the wind is blowing. You may see a weather vane on a roof. See the picture. **weath·er vanes**

world the earth: *Grandmother took a trip around the world.* **worlds**

Y y

yard the ground around a building: *You can play in the front yard.* **yards**

yell cry with a strong, loud sound: *He yelled when the door shut on his finger.* **yells yelled yell·ing**

young not old: *Young people like to run.*

weathervane

Z z

zoo a place to keep wild animals. See the picture. **zoos**

Word List

Unit 1
send 19
floor 19
everybody 19
most 19
trash 20
money 20
loaf 20
I'm 20
early 21
Thursday 21
doll 21
uncle 21
California 21
ever 21
seen 21
careful 22
corner 22
dinner 25
entire 25
held 26
dear 27

Unit 2
perfect 32
extra 32
even 32
flute 32
lesson 32
love 33
moment 33
believe 33
apple 34
knot 34
true 34
awful 34
gentle 35
direction 35

wait 37
carry 37
telephone 38
string 38
hug 38
rest 39
hammer 40
code 40
clear 40

Unit 3
young 43
trust 43
easily 43
number 44
clue 44
word 44
repeat 44
herself 44
reward 44
elephant 45
behave 45
treat 45
trunk 45
pedal 46
horse 47
flag 47
final 49

Unit 4
anybody 53
excite 57
camp 57
tent 57
explore 57
campground 57
lap 57

path 58
lost 58
fallen 58
picnic 58
fire 58
dishes 59
tired 59
idea 59
shadow 59
hoped 60
heard 60
forget 60
return 61
spaceship 62
robot 62
computer 62
landing 62
magnet 62
planet 62
stepped 64
glued 66

Unit 5
chipmunk 70
stream 70
log 70
bridge 70
bump 70
acorn 70
sack 70
understand 71
while 71
chat 71
disappoint 71
sulk 71
knock 72

292

Artists
Section 1: Elizabeth Allen, 9–13; Jim Conahan, 16; Susan Dodge, 29–31; Ann Iosa, 14–15; Nancy Munger, 43–49; Terry Pinkney, 19–27
Section 2: Jan Brett, 70–75; Brian Bourke, 62–67; Ted Carr, 54–56, 69; Robert Masheris, 52–53, 57–61, 76–81, 92; Sally Eckman Roberts, 84–91
Section 3: Jan Brett, 119–121; Yvette Marie Heyden, 94–95; Benton Mahan, 96–99; Robert Masheris, 110, 135; Ilse Plume, 124–133; Terry Sirrell, 134
Section 4: Yoshi Miyake, 136–137; William Peterson, 142–150; Christina Ljungren Rigo, 152–158; Terry Sirrell, 138–139; Ann Wilson, 160
Section 5: Elizabeth Allen, 192–202; Sharon Elzaurdia, 179–189, 191; Robert Masheris, 204, 210; Jerry Scott, 176–178; Slug Signorino, 174–175
Section 6: Marlene Ekman, 221–229; Paul Galdone, 246, 248–256; Robert Masheris, 259; Gretchen Mayo, 234–243; Yoshi Miyake, 216–217, 232–233; Margaret Sanfilippo, 218–220; Slug Signorino, 231
Glossary: Franz Altschuler, 260–272

Freelance Photography
Allan Landau, 205–213

Photographs
Page 82: Courtesy Holt, Rinehart & Winston; Page 100: (left) Courtesy Shelburne Museum, Shelburne, VT; Page 100: (center), Chalkware fireman, 1860–1900—Effie Thixton Arthur Bequest. Museum of American Folk Art; Page 100: (right), Courtesy Shelburne Museum, Shelburne, VT; Page 101: (top left), Manu Sassoonian/Art Resource, NY; Page 101: (bottom left), Spencer L. McConnell/BRUCE COLEMAN INC., New York; Page 101: (right), Elisa Leonelli/BRUCE COLEMAN INC., New York; Page 102: (left), Haga Collection, Tokyo; Page 102: (right), © Jack Vartoogian; Page 103: (left), Berg & Assoc./Gus Schonefeld; Page 103: (right), Sally Myers; Page 104: (top left), G. & G. Schaub; Page 104: (top right), Berg & Assoc./Gus Schonefeld; Page 104: (bottom left), Phil & Loretta Hermann/TOM STACK & ASSOCIATES; Page 104: (bottom right), G. & G. Schaub; Page 105: (left), Janice Ott; Page 105: (top right), © 1985—David H. Wells; Page 105: (bottom right), Museum of American Folk Art; Page 106: (top left), Albert Hilton; Page 106: (top center), Berg & Assoc./Margaret Westfall; Page 106: (bottom center), L. Cazzangi/Shostal Associates; Page 107: (left), Thomas Hovland from Grant Heilman Photography; Page 107: (right), Everett C. Johnson; Page 108: (top), Ray Hunold; Page 112: Bob Glaze/Artstreet; Page 113: Historical Society of Pennsylvania; Pages 114–116: Brown Brothers; Page 117: Peter Gridley/FPG; Page 118: Courtesy Jan Brett; Pages 119–121: © Jan Brett 1983. Courtesy of Sunrise Publications Inc.; Page 123: © Jack Vartoogian; Pages 161 (bottom), 166–170: Courtesy Kraft Inc.; Page 246: Courtesy Little, Brown & Company; Page 257: Photo by Rosanna H. Rosse. Courtesy Paul Galdone.

Cover Artist
Laura Lydecker